SOUL JOURNEY NUMBERS

YOUR GUIDE TOWARDS ENLIGHTENMENT

from

Jilly & Les

JILLY STOTT AND LESLÉ AYRE

Soul Journey Numbers

Published by MindStir Media, LLC

45 Lafayette Rd | Suite 181| North Hampton, NH 03862 | USA

1.800.767.0531 | www.mindstirmedia.com

Printed in the United States of America.

ISBN-13: 978-1-965340-17-2

Inspiration for the book
By Jilly Stott

Numbers have fascinated me throughout my life. I loved maths at school, I have studied and worked with feng shui and chinese astrology (I am a master of both subjects) for the past thirty plus years, which both work with numbers in different ways.

In 2014 I was drawn to visit the Ardèche region of France where I had stored a fabulous healing system in the twelfth/thirteenth century. This is called Source Energy Healing, and there are now many practitioners in the UK and abroad. This profound, yet very gentle healing has been returned to us now so that we can move forward in all areas of our lives, clear karma and energy blocks and heal our bodies at a deep cellular level.

During the Spring and Summer of 2018 I produced a set of 36 Source Energy Wisdom Guidance Cards with Leslé Ayre (one of my excellent Source Energy Healing practitioners and a dear friend), Kerry Beall, a very talented artist and graphic designer, the late and much missed John Davies, who formatted the guidebook that goes with the cards, and Peter, my husband, who is a tower of strength and a wonderful (very patient) proof reader.

This book is the next chapter on my Source Energy journey which I know you will find very interesting! It is different from other books on numbers in the same way that Source Energy Healing is different from any other form of healing that I, my practitioners or clients, have ever experienced.

My suggestion is that you approach this Source Energy Wisdom way of looking at numbers with fresh eyes, without comparing it with other numbering systems. It is different, it is unique, it will give you insights and wisdom to help you move forward on your own unique soul journey. It is a tool to help you, support you and guide you.

We run a unique course (one day a week for ten weeks, plus a weekend locally with us) so that you can fully assimilate all aspects of this fascinating book with deeper insights and wisdom.

Kerry and Peter, my husband, have once again worked closely with Leslé and me to produce this unique numbers book. Penelope and Christine joined us later to help with the proof reading.

Enjoy your Number adventure

Notes from the authors

When we wrote the first few drafts of this book, we had many, many capital letters and bold text! During the final stages of editing, when we were looking at the printed page, it felt too much to have so many initial capital letters and items highlighted, which made it difficult to read! In consultations with proof reading editors, we realised that we had to make some major changes. We have kept Source, God, Christ, Divine and Trinity as initial capitals, as well as Divine Feminine and Divine Masculine, Earth, the months of year and names.

We have lower case letters for source self, soul self, source light, sacred shape, spiritual being, vibration, soulmates, observer, pattern etc, as well as the shapes – the octahedron etc, and the power animals – dolphins etc. These are very important to us and to the wisdom within the book. We trust this format makes it easy for you to read.

Introduction

The Soul Journey Numbers Book: Your guide to discovering your true self. The soul journey numbers are sacred vibrations from the Source that help you understand the reality of who you truly are. You will feel empowered to move forward in your life with insight, confidence, and a deeper understanding of how to make decisions from your own innate wisdom, which we call our 'source self'.

The concept of Source typically refers to a fundamental, all encompassing force or energy from which everything in existence arises. In the context of this book, Source refers to the ultimate reality, or the highest state of consciousness that one seeks to realise or awaken to. It is the recognition of one's true nature or essence (source self) which transcends individual identity and ego (personality self) and instead experiences the interconnectedness and the profound sense of unity (oneness) with the universe.

This awakening of the Source Consciousness within is the process that we call Enlightenment.

The Source Consciousness within us already knows this great truth, however the soul growth comes from the mind overcoming the illusion of feeling that we are separate from Source. This is our evolving soul journey toward enlightenment.

The aim is to support you as you connect with your Source Consciousness.

This book is designed for you to dip in daily to help you connect with your source self, and explore how your date of birth and name influence your life purpose. Allow the wisdom of these power animals, sacred geometric shapes and masters to guide you throughout your days ahead.

We have marked in italics actions you can take to help yourself, or for emphasis.

As you embark on your journey of self discovery, there will be days where you may feel elated and experience a sense of clarity, and others where you may need to give yourself time to process your discoveries, so remember to be kind to yourself and embrace the present moment.

We look forward to hearing about your progress on your journey towards enlightenment.

with love and blessings

Jilly and Leslé

Soul Journey Numbers
Your Guide Towards Enlightenment

As we live our lives here on planet Earth, various soul awareness experiences occur. This soul journey numbers book and its guidance imagary are designed to help us with these experiences of awareness by giving us strategies to help us to move forward more easily on our own unique soul journey to Enlightenment.

Soul Journey Numbers

Soul journey numbers are sacred vibrations from Source.

They are part of the sacred geometry of Source, which is the language of Source. The understanding of the soul journey numbers will unlock certain aspects of our own source wisdom.

Use the vibration of numbers when you need wisdom or clarification.

The soul journey numbers are:

1   2   3   4   5   6   7   8   9   11

The soul journey numbers way of working with numbers is different from other numerological systems. You will notice that we have included the number eleven. This gives the system a greater depth of meaning.

This numbering system will help you to move forward in your life and on your own unique soul journey.

Please take your time to assimilate this new way of working with numbers. We are sure that you will find it fascinating, intriguing and illuminating.

THE NUMERIC PATTERNS OF SOURCE ENERGY
WITHIN EACH NUMBER

as shown in the soul journey guidance images

There are 39 images within the book (pages 170 to 208). You will notice that they follow in numeric order, one to nine, plus eleven. There are 33 numeric images, with a further 6 images (active awareness) representing sacred geometry.

Numeric Patterns of Source Energy

It is fascinating that each number has many patterns of energy, which we feel as energetic vibrations, these in turn draw particular situations and help towards us.

With this in mind you will see that after the number two there is a sub division of each number, as detailed below. Each sub division is a significant 'pattern of source energy' that is part of the whole soul journey number vibration. Each number has many vibrational patterns of energy, and each pattern adds a further insight into the soul journey number.

There are infinite patterns of energy within each number; however, we have brought forward those that have the most powerful influence on our lives at this significant time. Please note that the pattern of energy of, for example, (one+two) and (two+one) are similar, bearing in mind that the first digit has the bigger impact.

Soul Journey Number	Patterns of Source Energy (of the Soul Journey Number)			
One				
Two				
Three	One+Two			
Four	One+Three	Two+Two		
Five	One+Four	Two+Three		
Six	One+Five	Two+Four	Three+Three	
Seven	One+Six	Two+Five	Three+Four	
Eight	One+Seven	Two+Six	Three+Five	Four+Four
Nine	One+Eight	Two+Seven	Three+Six	Four+Five
Eleven	Two+Nine	Three+Eight	Four+Seven	Five+Six

Principal Numbers One, Two and Three

Take a moment to consider the soul journey numbers on this chart. What will stand out are the principle numbers of one, two and three; these are the vibrations of creation. **They are the creative principle numbers.**

The energetic signature of the number one is part of every vibrational pattern. As one is wholeness, which can also be seen as Source, then we can see that every number and its energetic patterns carry the wholeness of Source and the will of Source; **Divine Will.**

If we study this further, we can see the significance of the energetic signature of the number two in the energetic patterns of the soul journey numbers. The energetic signature of two is unconditional love: universal or **Divine Love.**

Finally, the creative principle number three is from the union of one and two. The signature of the vibration of three is also found in all subsequent energetic patterns of the soul journey numbers. The signature of this vibration is the knowledge of Source, which is complemented by love, this is **Divine Wisdom.**

Soul Journey and Soul Contract

Here is our definition of soul journey and soul contract. You may well have a different definition, which is fine. The images will work well for you whatever your definition.

Your intention is very important and defines the answers that you are given.

Soul Journey

Everybody is on their own unique soul journey. Each of our incarnations is an integral part of our own soul journey.

Our soul journey is infinite and this lifetime is a (small) part of our soul journey. These images will highlight what it is that we need, the gifts in this lifetime, and the lessons on our life journeys. For this incarnation our gifts can be seen as talents or positive qualities that our personality exhibits, our lessons seen as the challenges and difficulties that our soul has chosen to help us expand as beings of light.

The soul journey is about the bigger picture. It is about the eternal journey of our soul. The images highlight the energy that surrounds us at this particular part of our soul journey.

We are aiming to become more of what we are and to experience what we are through many incarnations, both on Earth and elsewhere. The ultimate aim of our soul journey is to come to terms with our fear based illusions, see our life from the reality of Source flowing through us to fully understand that we are a complete expression of Source.

Therefore, this aspect of our soul journey, this lifetime on planet Earth, is a very small part of our soul journey, which is why we have so much help and assistance from the universe, with the sacred shapes, power animals, masters etc. The soul journey is about the bigger picture, it is forever, it is our path to enlightenment.

The number for our soul journey consists of two digits. Our date of birth, that day that we have chosen to incarnate on planet Earth, gives us the two digits of our soul journey. These two digits represent the first and second stages of our journey in this lifetime. It is important to fully integrate the first stage before starting on the second stage.

The images help you to understand and integrate each stage. First with detailed help, then 'active awareness' action. The power animals, masters, crystals and colours add depth and meaning to help you move towards enlightenment.

Soul Contract

Our soul contract highlights what we need to focus on in this lifetime, the promise we have made to our soul, to the universe. What we are working on in this lifetime can be seen as a magnifying glass on the current part of our soul journey.

It helps us to notice those events through our life that have a similar pattern, helping us to move forward on our soul journey, releasing the fears and challenges to find the harmony and peace within and so the peace without. Peace is Source. When we face our soul contract with the help of our power animal, we are able to see the Source within.

Our fearful illusions are not part of us, or the real us. The more we can face these fears from a higher perspective the more opportunities there are for soul growth. We are constantly getting these soul contract opportunities, although we may not recognise them! The more honest we are with ourselves, the more we can embrace the opportunities and move forward.

Nothing is good or bad, it just is. We cannot 'run away'. It is time to work on our fears and challenges. Equally it is time to fully embrace our source filled positive qualities and talents.

Both our soul journey and our soul contract have power animals associated with them. The power animal for our soul journey is with us throughout our incarnations and the power animal for our soul contract is for this lifetime, and is there to help us through the challenges and fears, to enable us to move forward on our soul journey with love, strength and peace.

What to Notice in each Soul Journey Guidance Image

As well as a soul journey number you will notice that each image has a power animal, a master, a sacred shape, a crystal and a colour, please refer to the following table:

Number	Power Animal	Master	Active Awareness Sacred Shape	Crystal	Colour
One	Blue Whale	Melchizedek	Sphere	Clear Quartz	White
Two	Goldfinch and Eagle	Metatron	Two overlapping Spheres	Selenite	Iris Blue
Three	Dove	Sananda	Three overlapping Spheres	Citrine	Golden Yellow
Four	Deer	Mary and Joseph	Tetrahedron	Rose Quartz and/or Malachite	Rose Pink
Five	Jaguar	Kuthumi	Pyramid	Carnelian	Orange
Six	Swan	St Peter and Rosa	Octahedron	Desert Rose	Aqua Green
Seven	Dolphin	John the Baptist and Saint Germain	Seven Spheres Seed of Life	Blue Lace Agate and Amethyst	Wisteria Blue
Eight	Tiger + Red Admiral Butterfly	Moses	Star Tetrahedron	Red Jasper	Orange
Nine	White Husky + the Hare	Mary Magdalena and Tara	Octahedron surrounded by a Sphere	Labradorite and Moonstone	Mauve
Eleven	Snow Leopard	Maitreya	Twelve Pointed Star	Amethyst	Lavender Blue

The images can be found between pages 170 and 209. All aspects of each image are important. Therefore, when you have chosen your image (pages 11 and 114 will help you) take time to really appreciate and understand all the different aspects of your chosen image. Absorb every facet of the image. Which of the many features stand out the most for you?

If you have a crystal like the one mentioned on the image, you may like to hold it whilst you are working with your chosen image. Now pay particular attention to the power animal. Sit quietly and focus on this power animal and listen to the messages that you receive. Work with the master connected to this image. Be aware of the sacred shape and how this feels. Let it surround you. Sit within the shape and experience its energy and the help it is offering to you. Return your focus to the whole image, what it is telling you.

THE POWER ANIMALS

These power animals have stepped forward to help us on our soul journey:

The blue whale relates to the number one energy

The goldfinch and eagle relate to the number two energy

The dove relates to the number three energy

The deer relates to the number four energy

The jaguar relates to the number five energy

The swan relates to the number six energy

The dolphin relates to the number seven energy

The tiger and red admiral butterfly relate to the number eight energy

The white husky and the hare relate to the number nine energy

The snow leopard relates to the number eleven energy

Each individual explanation of the power animal will be found further on in the book, from page 138 to 157. They provide us with guidance on our soul journey and each carry the vibrational frequency of a soul journey number.

These magnificent power animals work to help us with our daily challenges, which can be seen as 'soul growth opportunities'. They help us to understand our lives; to move out of 'victim mode', identify situations that we need to look at and possibly clear and identify anything that needs to be released, including karma.

The power animal pages will show us qualities and traits that these power animals will help us with, including the qualities and traits that we still need to address.

It is our intention, which derives from our source self, that resonates with the individual frequency of these power animals and which will call on their wise loving qualities to help us.

It is important to note that every single living creature on this planet will resonate with one of these numbers. If we are drawn to a certain number and the power animal does not resonate with us, we can sit quietly and allow the Source within us to reveal the power animal that will help.

This is a huge Source filled gift that we have been made aware of; our gratitude will enhance and clarify the guidance that each power animal brings.

Each power animal has qualities and traits associated with it. The more we work with the power animals, our name and our soul contract, the stronger the positive qualities and traits become, and the less supportive traits and qualities are understood and released.

The White Owl

The white owl on the cover of this book (and page 209) symbolises wisdom from Source and represents the **concept of oneness.** The white owl helps us to understand that we are one with everything, and more importantly, helps us to remember this huge truth as we go through each day facing our challenges and fears.

The source filled energy of the white owl echoes around each of the power animals, reflecting how the energy of the number one is found in each of the other soul journey numbers.

If you are drawn to this book you have already been touched by the wisdom of the white owl. So embrace the wisdom of the white owl while exploring the following pages and allow its unfolding wisdom to help you on your journey to enlightenment. The white owl may come to you of its own accord through various signs. You may even see it in collections of numbers containing the numbers one and eleven.

Active Awareness Sacred Shapes

There are also six active awareness images (pages 203 to 208), which show the sacred geometric shapes of:

The Sphere	The Pyramid
The Octahedron	The Star Tetrahedron
The Twelve Pointed Star	The Seed of Life

Further details on each active awareness image can be found on pages 115 to 127.

Masters

When you are working with these soul journey guidance images, you may also choose to connect with the master working with that particular number set. The master will then bring with them special qualities connected to the images that will help your insights and general understanding. You may have worked with these masters in the past; however, as you will appreciate, these images work in a different way and the masters bring qualities with them to assist you when working with the images. For information on each master please refer to pages 158 – 161.

Crystals

There are crystals that work with all of these images. They work alongside the masters and the sacred shapes to bring added depth and wisdom to the individual images. For further information on the way that the crystals work with the images please refer to page 162.

Colours

There are also colours that correspond to each of the images, adding insights and understanding.

Using the Soul Journey Guidance Images

We have listed nine methods that we have found useful. There are unlimited ways of using these images, and once you have tried our nine methods please feel free to use your own with soul filled imagination.

Method one: Intuitive inspiration for the day (helping you to live in the present)

Method two: Soul journey (stage one and two, using your date of birth)

Method three: Soul contract number - using the Source Energy number pattern

Method four: Birth day number

Method five: How your name supports your soul journey

Method six: Further insights using yearly and monthly numbers

Method seven: Working with the power animals

Method eight: Working with the sacred geometric shapes – Active Awareness images

Method nine: Working with past lives

It is important to start with the first method as this gives you a good grounding and knowledge of the images and, when you are ready, you move on to methods two and three etc for deeper understanding of your own personal soul journey.

Whichever method you use, it is important that you take your time when choosing a soul journey guidance image, ensuring that you are well grounded and also being present.

Take some relaxing diaphragm breaths, breathing in gently through your nose, using your diaphragm so that more oxygen reaches your lungs, and then gently relaxing your diaphragm so that the breath is automatically gently exhaled once again through the nose. Continue breathing in this rhythm and feel yourself relaxing and being present in the moment.

We work a lot with the breath as it is one of the best ways to remain present and grounded in the moment.

Method One: Intuitive Inspiration for the Day
(Helping us to live in the present moment)

When you feel relaxed, think about the situation in your life that you would like help with. With your awareness allow the situation to come into your mind and gently observe it. Do not go into the drama of the situation.

When you are feeling relaxed, centred and ready you need to choose the image for the day, using the method detailed below (pages 10, 11 and 114).

When you have chosen your image, turn to the appropriate page in the book relating to that image (pages 17 to 83) and look at the image carefully. What does it initially tell you?

If you have chosen 'an active awareness image', then this particular sacred shape will help and support you throughout your day. You will find further information on these six sacred shapes on pages 115 to 127.

Read through the text about your chosen image with an open mind. Absorb the wisdom of the words. Take your time to fully appreciate and integrate what the words are telling you.

How are these words helping you to move forward? What steps can you now take to move your life forward on your own soul journey with love, integrity and wisdom?

Then turn to pages 101 to 110 relating to intuitive inspirations, and become aware of the additional help and support that is there for you.

You can use this method whenever you need additional help or guidance with any situation. You will find it very helpful.

How to use the Soul Journey Guidance Images Intuitively

There are various methods you can use to choose your guidance image. Choose one of these ways.

Thinking about your reasons for choosing the appropriate image, turn to the next page, choose the code that feels appropriate; this can be by moving your finger over the codes and then picking the one that feels appropriate; or if you are a dowser, you may like to dowse for the appropriate code; or you can follow your intuition and choose the right code.

Another way to choose the code is to choose a letter from A to Z and then a number from 1 to 3, this will give you the code for your image.

Know that you will choose the perfect image to help and support you.

When you have your code then turn to page 114 to see the image that the code relates to, and then turn to the appropriate image in the book.

H2	O2	L2
G1	N1	E1
R2	D1	Q1
S2	J1	H1
A1	M1	I3
V2	E2	R1
L1	T2	G2
Q2	W1	N2
O3	K1	C1
C2	U3	T1
Z3	A2	F2
Q3	S3	M2
D2	B1	K2
Y1	U2	X3
F1	P3	O1
Z1	V1	B2
Z2	H3	L3
I1	X2	P1
M3	D3	A3
J2	W2	R3
Y2	G3	I2
K3	V3	W3
Y3	N3	F3
X1	B3	U1
E3	S1	C3
T3	P2	J3

Refer to the chart on page 114 to find the relevant image.

Method Two: Soul Journey (Stage One and Two)

We are all on our own unique soul journey. The more insights we have the easier it is to move forward and accomplish what we are here to achieve.

Your full date of birth is the day that you incarnated on planet Earth, it is the day that you chose to be born. It is your own very special day and will help you to gain valuable insights into why you are here and what you have come to do.

Calculate your Soul Journey Number Stage One

Write down your full date of birth in numerical format, for instance if you were born on the 29 December 1999, then you would write 29.12.1999.

You then add all of these numbers together:

$$2 + 9 + 1 + 2 + 1 + 9 + 9 + 9 = 42$$

Therefore someone born on 29 December 1999 has the soul journey number 42.

If we then look at an older person, say born in 1940 during the second world war, on mid summer's day, 21 June 1940, and then add up these numbers we get

$$2 + 1 + 6 + 1 + 9 + 4 + 0 = 23$$

Therefore, this pensioner born on 21 June 1940 has the soul journey number 23.

A mother born on 30 June 1988

$$3 + 0 + 6 + 1 + 9 + 8 + 8 = 35$$

Therefore the Mother's soul journey number is 35

A father born on 2 February 1983

$$2 + 2 + 1 + 9 + 8 + 3 = 25$$

Therefore, the Father's soul journey number is 25

Double Numbers and their Significance

If your soul journey number is 11 then please go to the text about the number 11 on page 73. The number 11 is a very powerful number, it is very significant in itself.

If your soul journey numbers are the same, for instance 22, 33 or 44, then both the first and second stages of your soul journey are represented by the same number.

Therefore, your focus throughout your lifetimes is strongly on the one number, making it very strong and important. There is no deviation. You have one lesson. Your focus is on the one goal, the one aim, making it very significant. The challenges and the fears will follow the same pattern. Working with the power animals, sacred shapes, masters and crystals will help you to move forward on all levels, towards enlightenment.

For further information on the soul journey numbers please refer to pages 17 – 83 for the text and 170 – 209 for the images.

If your Soul Journey or Contract Number ends in Zero or is a Single Digit

The zero represents Oneness, all that is. The number zero represents the Divine, Source. If your soul journey/contract number ends in a zero then the first number is doubly significant, it represents your soul journey and the whole emphasis is on this first number.

When your soul journey number ends in zero, then your soul contract number is also the first digit of your soul journey number.

For instance if your soul journey number is 30, then the three is very significant for you through all your lifetimes. You are working with the vibration of the Divine Love, Divine Will and Divine Wisdom of Source Consciousness. Your understanding of oneness is very strong, and you are very focused on your path, your goal in life.

Occasionally this may feel 'too much' which can result in you turning away from your strong connection with Source, with the Divine, and going 'off track'.

Zero is infinite and when you are reminded of this through the zero in your soul journey number then this is a call for you to be aware of this in many of your lessons. This knowledge will help you to be objective, to see the difficulty/challenge from a higher perspective.

If you add together the digits in your date of birth and you get a single digit, for example, 3 January 2001, so 3+1+2+0+0+1=7, then your soul journey number is seven and your soul contract number is also seven.

How to Understand your Soul Journey Number

The soul journey number consists of two digits. They are both very significant. It is important that the first digit of the soul journey number is fully integrated and assimilated and when this is complete move on to work with the second digit of the soul journey number.

Please take time with this, it is not a race! If the first digit of your soul journey number is not fully integrated and assimilated then it will not be possible to fully work with and assimilate the second digit of the soul journey number, which would compromise the ability to achieve the soul goals.

The soul journey guidance images that accompany this book will help here.

Working with the First Stage of your Soul Journey

Take the first number of your soul journey number and then the appropriate image for that number, for instance the person born on 29 December 1999, has the first digit of their soul journey number as four therefore they need to look at the main image four page 174, which has the words 'connecting with Mother Earth' at the bottom of the image and page 25 with the details of image four. The image has a beautiful picture of a stag and connects with Mary and Joseph. The crystals associated with image four are both rose quartz and malachite. You will also notice that the sacred shape is a tetrahedron, a three sided pyramid.

Take your time to absorb the energy of the appropriate image for the first digit of your soul journey number, which in our example is four. Work with all aspects of it and also be aware of any messages or insights that come to you. It is always a good idea to write these down so that you can remember them in the future.

When you have worked with the appropriate image, in this case image number four, turn to the explanation within this book for the first digit of your soul journey number and read through the text.

Take your time to work with all aspects of the appropriate image text as well as working through the active awareness action and further action.

At the end of the text there is information about the power animals, sacred shapes and masters. Work with these energies too.

What have you learnt from this first stage about your own unique soul journey? What do you need to do to help yourself progress?

When you think you have completed this first stage, look again at the appropriate image, appreciating all the aspects of it; look again at the words that go with that image. Is there anything else you can use to help you?

Working with the Second Stage of your Soul Journey

When you have fully integrated and assimilated the first digit of your soul journey number it is time to look at the second digit.

If we look at the person born on 29 December 1999 again, then the second digit of their soul journey number is two. To help this individual to integrate and assimilate the other part of their soul journey they need to look at the image number two, where they will see the golden eagle and the goldfinch, along with two overlapping spheres (vesica piscis).

The crystals associated with the number two image are selenite and pyrite. The words at the bottom of this image are 'Source and Personality Self'.

When you have located your appropriate image for the second digit of your soul journey number, study the image carefully. What is it saying to you? What are the messages and insights that you are receiving? Is there one aspect of the image that you feel is more relevant to you? If there is, then spend time to work with this aspect. Take your time, allow your heart and source self to interpret the deeper meaning of this image.

When you feel this is complete, turn your attention back to the book and the relevant pages that describe this second digit of your soul journey number. There is a lot of information there; please take time to absorb and work with all parts of this image that are very important to you and your life.

What have you learnt about your own unique soul journey? What do you still need to do to progress on your soul journey?

Work with the active awareness action for that image so that you are fully integrating this second stage of your soul journey.

What are the insights, visions and promptings that working with this image has brought to the fore?

How can you integrate these to help you on your soul journey.

What have you learnt from working with both the first and second digits of your soul journey number?

What do you need to do so that both of these numbers have been fully integrated into your body and aura on all levels?

Plan how you are going to achieve this with the help that you receive from the image and the appropriate words.

Method Three: Soul Contract Number

When you have worked with both aspects of your two digit whole numbers that relate to your soul journey and have really integrated and assimilated your soul journey numbers, then it is time to look at your soul contract number.

Calculating your Soul Contract Number

Take the two digits from your soul journey number and add them together. It is the pattern of the whole number that is relevant to your soul contract.

Let us use the mother's example. She was born on 30 June 1988 and her soul journey number is three and five.

Therefore, to determine her soul contract number we add the numbers together, giving us the pattern $3 + 5 = 8$. Her soul contract number is the pattern three+five of the whole number eight, see page 59.

If we then look at her husband, who was born on 2 February 1983, his soul journey number is two and five. When we add these two numbers together $2 + 5 = 7$.

Therefore, his soul contract number is seven, which is made up of two+five – giving the soul journey seven (two+five) see page 49.

Let us also look at the person born on 29 December 1999, who has the soul journey number four and two. When we add these together we get $4 + 2 = 6$, therefore their soul contract number is six (two+four) see page 41.

In certain circumstances there is no pattern, for instance if the soul contract is 10, 20, 30 or 40. Just take the first digit, so 1 2 3 or 4, and understand that the zero represents the Oneness, the Source, the connection to the Divine.

SOUL JOURNEY GUIDANCE
ONE

Completion bringing new beginnings

Power animal: Blue Whale

Sacred shape: Sphere

Master: Melchizedek

Crystal: Clear Quartz

The power animal resonating with the vibration of the number one is the blue whale.

The shape that will help us to connect to the vibrational energy of the number one is a sacred sphere.

The crystal carrying the vibration of Melchizedek and the number one is clear quartz.

Each time a phase ends or a new cycle begins we will find that the vibration of the Number one is around us. The number one is constantly around us when we are working on plans and ideas to start a service to others.

In situations where we want or need to take a break, from either a work situation or a partnership, due to stress or unpleasantness, then the vibration of the number one will be drawn to us. At a soul level, this reminds us to move on, or change the present situation into one that causes less distress and unhappiness. It only needs our intent and awareness to connect to this vibration on a conscious level.

The vibration of the number one surrounds us when we are ready to take firm steps on our divine pathway. This can mean it is time for us to make a stand, to take life affirming forward steps with a feeling of empowerment. By being honest and true to ourselves through our words and actions, we will also be helping others to find their own authenticity.

We are aware of the vibration of the number one when we are being helped to claim our mastery and lead with courage. We may be called upon to be a leader in a work or social situation, which may initially feel unsettling; however, the energy of the number one is guiding us in the right direction, the direction we are meant to be following. Listen carefully and work from the heart.

If the vibration of one is prominent within your birth date numbers, you will understand others fears but not mirror them. You will be able to lead from a place of vision.

When we draw this image, this is our higher self prompting us to look inwards, into our divine self, for the new beginning, the next step on our own unique divine pathway. We will find that the energy of the number one will help empower us with the courage to step forward with integrity and strength.

We will find that the energy of Melchizedek will help us in the same way.

Active Awareness Action

Take time each day to find the truth of who you are, by tuning into the vibration of number one.

Place a sacred sphere of light around you with the intention that it is filled with the truth of who you are.

Allow your feelings of gratitude and anticipation to fill your thoughts. Immerse yourself in the sensation of having this sphere around you. Each time you do this you will find that your experience becomes more of a sensation than just a knowing. This action helps you to always speak from your heart.

Take time to do this, all the time using your breath to hold you in the present by concentrating on each measured diaphragm breath. This is your own rhythm of source breath, the breath of Source.

Hold a clear quartz crystal, which will help you to connect to Melchizedek and the vibration of the number one. Cleanse your crystal through intent and the Source within (use your breath). Dedicate your crystal to help you to be your true self and in your source power.

Further Action

Find a quiet place and feel yourself grounded and then, using your breath, breathe in the pure white light of Source. Remember to use the rhythm of source breath that is perfectly right for you. Ask Source for guidance for your next new phase. Spend time and allow the insights to come to you. This is something that you can do many times, and each time you will have a deeper understanding of your source filled future.

Power Animal

The blue whale resonates with the number one.

If you are drawn to this power animal, sit quietly in your sphere and allow the wisdom of the blue whale to surround you. This mighty mammal will help you to recognise your strengths and fears. You may be inclined to see your fears as expressions of weakness in your everyday existence. Rather, see your weaknesses as learning opportunities and your strengths as source filled wisdom and so be able to look at the next phase in your life through your source self.

New phases are opportunities for soul growth.

SOUL JOURNEY GUIDANCE
TWO

Source and personality self

Power animals:	Golden Eagle and Goldfinch
Sacred shape:	Two Interlocking Spheres
Master:	Metatron
Crystal:	Pyrite and Selenite

The power animals resonating with the vibration of the number two are the golden eagle and the goldfinch.

The sacred shape that will help us to connect to the vibrational energy of the number two, is two interlocking spheres.

The crystals that carry the vibration of Metatron and the number two are pyrite and selenite.

All relationships attract the vibration of the number two.

Where there are two energies that are drawn together and resonate beautifully with each other, or even if they clash, this is the vibration of the number two. The relationship between our soul self and our ego personality is the greatest relationship that we, as beings of Source, will ever have.

As we grow in awareness as a spiritual being, we will draw in the vibration of the number two which helps us to face our challenges and blocks. The yearning we might feel that nothing material satisfies us, or even the loneliness we can feel in a crowd, is our unconscious need to be connected to our source self. This will be our source self prompting us through the vibration of the number two to become aware that we are more than our personality self, that we are a source being on a journey of discovery through our material self.

When we are awake to this awareness it will give us freedom from loneliness (loneliness is one of the strongest expressions of fear). Instead, we will discover that we are never alone, that we are always at one with all.

When we draw this image we might be prompted to look at ourselves and see where we feel out of alignment. *Examine the type of thoughts and feelings that you have on a regular basis.* Our emotions are also an expression of our soul. If we often feel anger and/or fear, this can indicate that we are having difficulty staying in the present. The vibration of the number two will help us to stay in the present moment, enabling us to detach from anger and fear so that we do not respond so quickly to emotional patterns of behaviour.

Now is the time to focus on what we are thinking. Confront the thoughts that are fuelled by fear or anger. This will help us to understand our emotions or outbursts. It is time to be honest with ourselves and look at our lives.

Think about the times when you have felt joy, contentment and peace. Then think about what makes you feel upset, irritated, alone or afraid. These are emotional promptings from our soul self, so that we can appreciate what brings us peace and what it is that brings us unrest.

Drawing this image shows that we are ready to face changes in our lives, to become more in alignment with our soul, our source self, to look at the relationship between our source self and our personality self. This takes courage and a commitment to our soul journey.

Active Awareness Action

Write down the emotion, or emotions, that leave you feeling unsettled. Now write down the thought that created that emotion. Is this a regular thought during your day? How far back in your past have you been emotionally charged by this thought? If you feel you have an affinity with Metatron call in their energy and they will help you to make a strong connection to the source energy vibration of the number two.

Further Action

Place yourself into the centre (vesica piscis) of the two interlocking spheres of source light. Sit quietly and breathe in the pure white source light, feel it filling your entire body. Do this for a few minutes and make sure you keep bringing your focus back to the source light through being aware of your breathing.

Stay in this place of source vibration and allow yourself to face your true self. Now, once more look at the emotion, or emotions, that are leaving you feeling unsettled and allow your source self to flow through you as you write down the answers. Reflect on what is perhaps hidden in your deep subconscious. Allow your soul self to speak and gently guide you to understand your fears and thus understand your resultant emotions.

Power Animal

The golden eagle and the goldfinch resonate with the number two.

If you feel drawn to the golden eagle, surround yourself with its powerful energy. Allow the energy of the golden eagle to help you to soar above your fears and doubts and look at them from the state of being an observer, free of judgement yet filled with the perception and wisdom of one that loves unconditionally.

Alternatively, you may be drawn to surround yourself with the gentle soft energy of the goldfinch, who will stay with you allowing you to feel safe and free from the restrictions of limitations. With this guidance you will find yourself able to sit safely as the observer and watch your personality self through eyes that are free from judgement.

Freedom is awareness of Source.

SOUL JOURNEY GUIDANCE
THREE

Love, will and wisdom in the moment

Power animal:	Dove
Sacred shape:	Three Interlocking Spheres
Master:	Sananda
Crystal:	Citrine

The power animal resonating with the vibration of the number three is the dove:

> The white dove of peace
> The white dove of fulfilment
> The white dove of universal truth

The shape that will help us to connect to the vibrational energy of the number three is three interlocking spheres.

The crystal carrying the vibration of Sananda and the number three is citrine.

The number three vibrates with the love, the will and the wisdom of Source Consciousness.

When we are aware of the Divine Love, Divine Will and Divine Wisdom within us it enables us to see these Divine vibrations in others. Every day we have opportunities to understand the love, will, and wisdom of Source and to act through these vibrations of consciousness. This is our soul wanting to express itself in our life.

Our material life can often confuse and deter us from seeing the best in others or ourselves or perhaps keep us from understanding different actions or words from others or why we repeat the same harmful behavioural actions.

This is when we will draw the vibration of the number three towards us. Please understand that although like attracts like, it is our source self's desire to change the imbalance that in fact draws in the vibration of three.

This guidance image, with the vibration of three, is a soul prompting that perhaps the balance of love, will and wisdom is out of alignment with our soul self. Our confusion in trying to understand what is happening in our lives needs to be looked at from our source self where we are in perfect alignment. This will help us to be in tune with our loving self, our wise self and the **blueprint of Divine Will** that is our goal, our karma, our soul journey. Only in the present moment are we truly in alignment with our divine self will and so to the love and wisdom within.

Drawing this vibrational number three image indicates that it is time to take note of how often we are spending our time in the present moment.

Do you daydream about the future but take no actions towards its fulfilment?

Do you spend time thinking about past actions?

We can take a big step today and consciously intend to keep ourselves in the present as much as we can. It is only by being mindful or present that we can be aware of our loving self, our Divine Wisdom and then, with a clarity, have a deeper understanding about our earthly life.

Active Awareness Action

Focus on your breath. When you are aware of your breath you are in the present. Be aware of your surroundings. Hear, see and experience all that is going on around you. Place yourself into the centre of three interlocking spheres. Call for the golden light of Sananda to surround you and either find a quiet space to sit, or go on a quiet peaceful walk. Allow your source self to guide you to find your true divine self. Trust what you feel and think during this reflective time. You can do this by breathing each sphere into your awareness until you are in the centre of these three overlapping spheres. Now continue to concentrate on your breath until you find that quiet infinite peace that is within. The harmonised energy of the three spheres will help you to experience the Source within. You will feel the bliss of your source self. This will help you to move forward from a place of spiritual equalibrium.

Further Action

Call for the golden light of peace to surround you and either find a quiet space to sit, or go on a peaceful walk. Allow your source self to guide you to find your true divine self. Trust what you feel and think during this quiet time. Understand that what you feel and think are pointers to what you need to know to bring clarity and understanding to why you sometimes feel conflicting emotions.

Be continually mindful for at least three consecutive days of the vibration of three, the light of Sananda and the feeling of peace. This will help you to accept and love yourself and so be in touch with your wise self and thus able to see more clearly your next step in life.

Power Animal

The dove resonates with the number three.

If you choose to connect to this power animal then call in and connect to the white dove of peace, call in and ask to connect to the white dove of fulfilment and finally call in and connect to the white dove of universal truth.

Allow their love, guidance and wisdom to fill your inner heart space. Hear their wisdom from that inner space in your heart. Allow yourself to be open to any promptings, thoughts or insights that help you to see how to step forward in gratitude, peace and, in the awakening awareness, the will of your source self.

Just being brings peace.

SOUL JOURNEY GUIDANCE
THREE

source energy pattern
ONE + TWO

Family Interactions

The moment we arrive on our planet Earth most of us are part of a family and so are responsible for more than just ourselves. It can be joyous and wonderful to be blessed into a loving family but there are times when our blessings may be harder to see or understand.

Our biggest soul growths are through family relationships and when this happens we attract the number three in the pattern of one+two. Being true to ourselves is an essential part of family interaction.

Single parents will find that this pattern of the number three is around them in order to help them fulfil both parenting roles. This is a challenge for both the single parent and the child/children. However, it must be understood that this was prearranged and that, once more, huge soul growth is possible for all concerned. If we are attracting this pattern then perhaps we are feeling in a place of antagonism towards a family member or are feeling misunderstood. An example would be: As a child we may have had emotions of anger or unrest but we were ignored, which can result in us now finding it hard to communicate with siblings or even our own children.

Any feelings of emotional unrest within our family will benefit from understanding why we feel the way we do. We could draw this guidance image towards us as a parent who feels that our own needs are not being met, or are not being heard, or perhaps we are not able to understand our family's hostility.

This vibrational source energy pattern will be drawn towards us when we feel that either we have no voice in our family or, without being aware, we are not listening to others voices. Ask yourself:

Do I feel trapped?
Do I feel unheard?
Do I feel resentful in any way?
Do I feel unloved or unappreciated?

This is about our role in the family; how we feel about it and whether we are happy in it. Now that you have thought about these questions take time to see if you have unconsciously placed yourself into victimhood. This is very easily done especially when we are in a place of unresolved issues that we may not want to face. It is often easier to find the cause of our unhappiness outside ourselves than to take responsibility for our circumstances.

This inner searching takes huge courage and commitment. We need to take charge of our lives by examining our thoughts. How much awareness do we give to thoughts that carry fear, anger or suffering? It often helps to change our habitual negative thought patterns by looking at our lives from a different perspective.

With this in mind take time to take part in the active awareness action.

Active Awareness Action

Spend time writing down how you feel about your family members. What is it about your family that fills you with contentment, even joy? Now write down what you feel you would like to change.

Visualise yourself, and your family members, in the central interlocking space of the three spheres, feel the pattern one+two surround you with its golden light and allow yourself to be filled with gratitude for your family, firstly for the joy they bring and then for the gifts, in the form of challenges, they have given you in order for you to become a more enlightened being. Walk through your day being constantly aware of feelings and thoughts. Write down your thoughts in a notebook. You may like to do this for three days and then compare your notes and see how they differ over the three days. Each day your understanding will grow of why you are in your family and what commitments, which can be seen as gifts, you can give to your family and in turn what they can give to you.

Power Animal

The dove resonates with the number three.

If you feel drawn to the dove, surround yourself in the gentle energy of the white dove of peace (an aspect of the white dove). Experience how free you feel! Free from judgements. You find yourself coming into the space of being able to forgive. Experience how peaceful you feel and from that peaceful space forgive yourself. In time know that from a deep understanding of what your family members bring to you, the act of forgiveness becomes an act of giving and receiving with love.

Relationships are the greatest soul lessons.

SOUL JOURNEY GUIDANCE
FOUR

Connecting with Mother Earth

Power animal:	Deer (Doe and Stag)
Sacred shape:	Tetrahedron
Masters:	Mary and Joseph
Crystal:	Rose Quartz and Malachite

The power animal resonating with the vibration of the number four is the deer (the doe and the stag).

The shape that will help us to connect to the vibrational energy of the number four is a tetrahedron (a triangular pyramid with four equal triangular faces).

The two crystals carrying the vibration of Mary and Joseph and the number four are rose quartz and malachite.

The vibration of the number four and the source energy patterns it holds is all about Mother Earth, our connections with Mother Earth, how we interact with her energy, including the times that we work with her elements.

When we attract the vibration of number four we are being prompted to make sure our awareness is in the present moment at all times.

One of the best ways of doing this is to become aware of our physical body. We can do this through our breath and by focusing on various areas of our body. This can be done through a relaxing meditation or just a few minutes of intent. This process is very grounding. We need to understand that to be grounded we have to be present and if we are present in our awareness then we are in a state of Source Consciousness.

Another way of doing this is by connecting to Mother Earth in a more conscious way. Spending more time in nature will help with this awareness. If we are drawn to nature we will always attract the vibration of the number four, especially when we are creating a garden, or considering how to plan or landscape a garden. We need to take time to understand what the garden wants and what it needs to be in a state of harmony.

This can be done intuitively, perhaps by dowsing or even relying on what we are feeling when we look at various plants. A wonderful way is to 'body dowse'. This means we use our body to provide the answer. When the answer is positive we lean very slightly forwards and if the answer is negative we lean very slightly backwards. There may be a side to side motion when the answer is ambiguous.

An example: Hold a plant and go to the area you feel you would like to do the planting. Ask whether this will be a suitable spot for the plant and allow your body to respond.

The movement is a soft sway, sometimes almost imperceptible, however the more you use your body the more you will be in tune with your plants and your garden.

This method can even be used when considering what type of soil to use or how much sunlight is needed.

It is important to remember that when we have the intention of creating anything to do with Mother Earth we will draw towards us the vibration of the number four. Being aware of this will help us to understand the garden's needs.

Active Awareness Action

Fill your garden with the vibration of love and gratitude.

You may want to call in the energy of Mary's and Joseph's unconditional love and allow and intend this love to flow through your hands as you tend to your garden.

Feel how the garden responds to you. You are interacting with the vibration of the number four which is filled with the loving healing energy of Mother Earth.

Allow the garden to communicate to you what it needs and where are the best places to sit or even lie down.

Use your garden as a sanctuary of blessings which you receive each time you go out into the space that you have helped to create.

Further Action

If you do not have a garden but need plants around you then consider indoor plants. Think of them as new members of your family and spend time looking for the perfect area to place them.

Visualise a tetrahedron around your plants and a rose quartz or malachite crystal (or any crystal that feels right) close by. What you are creating with your intent is a rejuvenating regenerating pattern of energy.

The vibration of the number four is the perfect vibration for the physical healing of our bodies through being in the present moment and connecting to the love of Mother Earth.

Power Animal

The deer resonates with the number four.

Visualise a stag and doe in your garden with you. Feel how wonderfully grounded they are and feel grounded yourself. Spend time with the deer in your garden and feel the balance that they are bringing to you. Sit with the deer, both the stag and the doe, and see harmony within your garden and visualise exactly where you need to place your plants. Ask for the doe to care for your plants and shrubs and fill them with love.

Appreciating Mother Earth is fundamental to who we are.

SOUL JOURNEY GUIDANCE
FOUR

source energy pattern
ONE + THREE

Regenerate and Rejuvenate with nature

This source energy pattern vibration is especially strong in the Spring. From a Source perspective we are constantly regenerating (just like our gardens). Although this is being done constantly we are more aware of it during the Spring months when our soul is prompting us to link to this powerful force. Sitting or walking in nature is powerfully rejuvenating and we may be drawn intuitively to certain flowers, shrubs and trees that have a source essence healing vibration that will help us physically, mentally, emotionally and spiritually.

Gratitude for the beauty and wonders of these plants and trees helps us to link to the vibrational pattern one+three and connects us to whatever we are drawn to. There is healing potential in every shrub, tree and flower. Allow your source self to guide you. Each time we walk through nature, we can connect with and become the Earth, so that we blend with her and her heart energy. When we allow our physical senses to fill us with the sounds and smells of Mother Earth, we connect to her power, her rejuvenating and regenerating source vibration. This is a powerful way to become aware of Mother Divine and it is our gratitude and huge love for her that fills us with the pure source regenerating energy that connects us to all that is.

Active Awareness Action

Sit in an etheric tetrahedron (out in nature if possible). Be aware of the four equal faces (three around you and one below you). Become aware of your body by breathing in the energy of the tetrahedron. You are connecting with the energy of four. Feel your body glow and tingle with life. Connect with your source self through your inner heart. From this space visualise that every cell in your body is being regenerated with a source blueprint of perfection. Spend time doing this every day for a few days and feel how alive and full of energy you feel.

Further Action

Call in the energy of Source to help you to create a balance of source perfection within your body. Feel yourself filled with gratitude for all that this wonderful body of yours does for you. Mary or Joseph will help you with this.

This can be done in a short morning and evening meditation. In the morning intend that your day will be filled with love and think of a list of things or people that fill your life with happiness.

In the evening sit for a short time and remember even the smallest happenings that brought comfort or happiness to you. Allow yourself to be flooded with the sensation of wellbeing and gratitude.

This will help you to regenerate all aspects of yourself and to be in control of your thoughts and stop reacting to (mirroring back) the negative emotions of others. Mary and Joseph will help with this. You are then able to step back and detach and therefore respond in a positive way. You will also be helped to ground in a deep way by being aware of the temple that is your body from the higher perspective of source self.

From this space see your body being whole and in perfect working order. Allow the essence of life to fill and flood your body with the healing vibration of the number four in the pattern of one+three.

Working in this way helps us to understand the harmony and balance of source energy that is always in our body, the mother and father divinity that is present in every cell and all we have to do is to become conscious of this.

Working with Mary and Joseph will helps us to achieve this.

Power Animal

The deer resonates with the number four.

If you are drawn to this power animal you will be surrounded by its gentle energy. The deer will help you to understand why you may not always treat your physical body with love and gratitude, which causes your cells to be out of ease, so dis-eased.

Decide which energy is right at this particular time, either the soothing loving energy of the female doe or the trusting compassionate energy of the male stag.

Spend time in the energy and wisdom of this power animal by listening to the wind, the rustling of the trees, as you feel yourself blending with the vibrational pattern one+three. This will help you to feel how in tune you are to your body's blueprint of perfection, to the Divine Mother within and without.

Be grateful to Mother Earth every day.

SOUL JOURNEY GUIDANCE
FOUR

source energy pattern
TWO + TWO

Trust your Source Self

This vibrational pattern is drawn towards us when trust has become an issue. This includes trusting ourselves, trusting our body, our thoughts and our feelings. When we become more aware of our spiritual selves we are often drawn to gurus, spiritual leaders and counsellors who tell us to trust in ourselves.

What is trust?

To trust is to feel safe and in harmony with our decisions, choices and our thoughts. This in turn leads us to those who we know we can trust. To trust others we first need to trust ourselves. We need to be sure that in any situation or relationship where trust is called for we will act in a trustworthy way with integrity. The problem arises when we are not in control of our thoughts, our mental process, and therefore not in control of our emotions, which can sometimes take us by surprise! If we are not able to prevent ourselves from reacting to a low vibrational emotion then how can we trust ourselves, or trust that we will always respond in a healthy way that is for our greater good and soul growth. This can lead us to attracting the same trust issues in someone else.

Choosing this image and the pattern of two+two of the number four may also indicate that you need to ask yourself the following:

Do I feel good about the choices I make?   Do I trust my choices?
If not, is it because I rely on others to help me make decisions as I do not always trust myself?

Remember other people will always give advice from their perspective and although it can be very helpful, the most trustworthy decision will always come from our higher self. To do this we do need to be in touch with our source self and in the highest vibration possible. This in turn helps us to access the facts and the knowledge that we need to make the decision or choice.

Trust issues are almost always brought forward in relationships and it is here that we can learn about what trusting in someone else or even in trusting ourselves actually means to us. In some partnerships it may be that integrity, honour and respect are a natural foundation for the continuing relationship but for others it can mean the constant changing of partners in order to find that trust.

This seldom works as we have to start with building a foundation of integrity, grace and love within. This takes honesty and a journey of self love and the subsequent discovery that we need to start from trusting that we are Source.

As such we learn to move away from actions that create deceit. We will then attract what we are and trust will become the natural outcome of a relationship built from our own grace filled selves.

Active Awareness Action

The next time you need to trust yourself with a decision or perhaps a thought process, connect to your source self by bringing yourself into the present moment. A good way to bring yourself into the present moment is to concentrate on your breath; using your own source filled rhythm of breath is very effective and powerful. Breathe pure source light into your auric field, filling yourself with awareness of Source.

Now allow your choices to play out in front of you as if on a screen. See each choice as a reality that is happening, allow it to unfold. Feel yourself surrounded by the emotions and feelings you would experience with this choice. You may like to write them down. Now move onto your next choice and repeat the process. Now trust the choice that you are drawn to. If it is free from fear it is a prompting from your higher self. This is a big step towards learning to trust your higher self.

This is one of the most beautiful ways of learning to trust ourselves completely. That first 'knowing' that fills us is our source self prompting us for our higher good.

Power Animal

The deer resonates with the soul journey number four.

If you are drawn to this power animal surround yourself with the gentle energy of a deer. Allow yourself to merge with the energy of the deer. Feel how alert you feel, aware of every rustle and sound in the open space of nature, feel how the deer instinctively responds to different smells, sounds and movements.

This is perfect trust.

Spend time with this loving power animal and learn to trust.

Trust comes from being in your source self.

SOUL JOURNEY GUIDANCE
FIVE

Love yourself

Power animal: Jaguar

Source shape: Four sided pyramid with a square base

Master: Kuthumi

Crystal: Carnelian

The power animal resonating with the vibration of the number five is the jaguar.

The shape that will help us to connect to the vibrational energy of the number five is a four sided pyramid with a square base.

The crystal that carries the vibration of Kuthumi and the number five is carnelian.

We do not just attract the vibration of the number five, we are the vibration of five on a three dimensional level. As we are Source filled beings of light, living and experiencing a three dimensional life in a three dimensional body, this is a very important vibration to keep in perfect harmony.

Certain aspects of our bodies show clearly that we are part of the vibration of five. We have five fingers and five toes. We have five major appendages to our torso; the head, two arms and two legs. We also have five sense organs, sight, hearing, touch, taste and smell. All of this shows how we, when we are in our physical three dimensional body made from the components of Mother Earth, are the vibration of five.

It is often the inadequacies of our physical body that bring to us the greatest soul growth and evolvement. First, we must remember that the perception of these inadequacies is subjective and that in another culture or background we may not consider a particular perceived fault as being so. Secondly it is how we respond to the subjectively perceived physical inadequacy of our physical body. This is often subject to our feelings of self worth. These feelings of self worth may be affected by today's material world and the huge hold that the media has over us in regard to the expectations of physical perfection.

When we are drawn to this image, it is a reminder that we chose this beautiful vessel and although it may not always be what we feel we want, it may be time for us to see ourselves with eyes that are filled with gratitude and love.

This act of gratitude is a source filled grounding action and as gratitude can only be expressed in the moment, it helps us to ground with Mother Earth and have a strong connection to Source.

We may need to start re-evaluating how we feel about our physical body or how we treat our physical body.

Do you feel dissatisfied with your body?
Perhaps we would be happier if it was a different shape or size?

It is very easy to see what we do not like, but maybe it is time to own our body, to accept and love our body.

Look at what our body does for us; be grateful for what it does for us and from this gratitude listen to what our body needs.

Does your body need more exercise?
Do you need to change your diet?
Do you need to drink more water?

Active Awareness Action

Place yourself in a four sided pyramid, being aware of the square base. (In this way you are within a shape that has five sides around you.) Feel **the light of Source** *pouring through the uppermost point of the pyramid, flooding your energy centres with source healing, at the same time being aware of your physical body. You may wish to call in the energy of Kuthumi to help you.*

Allow gratitude to fill you in appreciation of everything your body has done for you. Imagine the inside of the pyramid having mirrors and look at yourself with acceptance and then love. From this loving space ask your body what you can do to help it into a better state of wellbeing. You will receive answers!

Further Action

Call on your higher self to help you on your journey of physical wellbeing. A good way to do this is to hold a piece of carnelian while siting within an etheric four sided pyramid. Hold the carnelian in the centre of your body and feel the sun's light pouring from the carnelian into the centre of your body, so that it fills your entire body with light. Now feel that light as love for yourself. Sit in this love for yourself and absorb it into all the cells of your body. Finally remember you are not the body, you are infinite Source expressing life through a physical body that is perfect for the lessons and the joy you will experience.

Power Animal

The jaguar resonates with the number five.

If you feel drawn to this power animal, call for the energy of the jaguar to surround you. Close your eyes and become the jaguar, feel how attuned you are to this powerful animal, feel how in sync this power animal is to its physical body. Spend time experiencing how joyful it feels to be in tune with a physical body.

Keep this joyous feeling of Source and material union and return to your own body. You will feel so alive. Spend time sitting quietly, being aware of each part of your body, all the time being linked to the insightful energy of the power animal, the jaguar.

Our body is the vehicle for our highest soul experience.

SOUL JOURNEY GUIDANCE
FIVE

source energy pattern
ONE + FOUR

We are Beings of Light

When we draw this particular pattern of five towards us it is because we have woken up to the fact that we are a Being of Source Light experiencing life through a material body. Once this concept is understood, our journey to enlightenment has begun.

In understanding this it also means that a huge responsibility has come into being. We are responsible for how we use this material body. We are responsible for our body's wellbeing.

One of the biggest challenges we face when we understand that we are a spiritual being is not wanting to be part of the everyday chaos that a material life brings to us. We may want to stay in that place of meditation, trance or wonderful uplifting visualisation, which can be easier than addressing life and its physical challenges. It may feel easier to ignore our physical bodies needs and this can in turn affect how we see other physical beings.

We may be drawn to this particular image because we do not always identify our body as being part of spirit. If we do not see this in ourselves we will have little regard for the physical material forms of others. When this happens, it is harder to understand what our body needs or even to take part in the energy healing of our body or participate in the energy healing of others.

Our bodies are spirit in a denser material form and thus once we engage in this understanding we are able to experience life in a constant state of harmony and able to attract a future that is perfect for our soul growth.

To understand the wonder of the material body is to first understand who we truly are and then embrace this material extension of our spiritual self. This is awareness.

The vibration of the number five is at its strongest when we feel gratitude for our human body; however when we call in the pattern of one+four then we are understanding that each cell in our body is filled with Source or Life and that we can, as a spiritual being, identify with each cell or molecule of water in our body.

Active Awareness Action

Sit quietly in a place where you will not be disturbed. Close your eyes and concentrate on your breathing until you feel relaxed and in the moment. You may feel drawn to connect to Kuthumi's powerful energy.

Now open your eyes and look at your feet, breathe light into them. Think of how many steps they have taken in your lifetime! Now move your attention to your legs and once more breathe light into them and in your mind see how they have held you erect, allowed you to run, climb, march and have taken you wherever you have wanted to go. Allow yourself to feel the wonder of this.

Work through as many parts of your physical body that you feel drawn to. The hands are very important in this exercise. When you have breathed light into each limb, allow yourself to marvel at the complex movements that you take for granted. This is bringing your awareness and gratitude into each part of your body. Love and admire what your body can do rather than what it cannot do. This is especially true for those that have physical challenges.

This action can be done for your limbs and you can also include your internal organs. Do what feels right for you in the moment. This is a very powerful awareness action and if done regularly will bring huge positive changes to your life.

Further Action

Visualise yourself in an energetic four sided pyramid with a square base. This will help you to connect to the pattern of one+four, which in turn will help you to fully understand the concept of just being. Spend time doing this whenever life feels chaotic and out of control.

This will help you to understand the wondrous concept that when you allow yourself to be in that space of being you are detached from the ego personality that identifies itself with the body.

You are pure Source Energy.

Power Animal

The jaguar resonates with the number five.

If you are drawn to this power animal, step into its energy, feel yourself blend with the energy of this intuitive, clear seeing power animal. Spend time being aware of how you can look at your personality self's difficulties and fears with clear seeing eyes. Feel how you step instinctively into your true self, allowing you to be conscious of what your source self is communicating to you.

This is enlightenment.

Enlightenment is a state of Being.

SOUL JOURNEY GUIDANCE
FIVE

source energy pattern
TWO + THREE

Harmony within reflecting harmony without

The pattern of the two+three aspect of the number five is indicative of how we connect with our inner feelings and how that makes us act. This is about the relationship between our actions and our feelings. We will draw this image to us when we find that we are not in control of some of our reactions.

We feel anger and hit out. We feel sadness and often cry. We feel grief and our actions are uncaring and thoughtless. All of these extreme feelings can lead to emotional outbursts, emotional irrationality and perhaps lead to unwise actions.

Why is this?

This is often because our feelings are so powerful and yet we feel we must suppress them for whatever reason. This can lead to emotional outbursts that are not always intended.

The vibrational pattern of the two+three aspect of the number five helps us to connect to the underlying feelings that we have perhaps buried and that need to be aired. We need to see why we react strongly instead of responding in a manner relevant to an outside stimulus. The harmonious relationships between our mind, our feelings and our body are a pure source connection as all three are, in fact, aspects of Source and when they are in harmony we will feel our true source self.

The first action is not to judge our emotional outburst and subsequent actions. The second action is to take steps to understand.

One way to do this is to give ourselves the gift of time and the intention to understand. Sometimes it is quite obvious, but we may need to spend time connecting to our higher self, raising our own vibration and allowing our higher self to enlighten us. Kuthumi will help us with this. It may even require us to go to a person who is perhaps trained in helping us to discover our subconscious hidden thoughts and memories that cause our intense feelings.

The key thoughts here are:

Free yourself from guilt.
Do not judge your actions, rather detach and observe the thoughts.
Forgive yourself through understanding.

All of these actions will help this vibrational number pattern to ease us towards a strong harmonious relationship between our mind, feelings and body. Lord Kuthumi will always help us when we are taking steps of enlightenment and by becoming aware of the need to understand why we react in a way that suggests we are not in harmony with our source self. This will mean that we are becoming more spiritually aware.

Active Awareness Action

You may choose to visualise yourself surrounded by a four sided energetic pyramid on a square base. Use your own rhythmic source breath to help you to be in the present. Allow your higher self to present to you the emotions you feel that cause you pain. Write them down. Now from a place of detachment write down how often you feel these emotions. Write down what or who causes you to feel like this. Sit quietly and allow your higher source self to deepen your understanding. Remember you are not judging, you are merely observing and in doing so you may notice a pattern of behaviour. Observe the pattern of behaviour and see how far back it goes. Allow time for this.

An early memory of the behavioural pattern will come to the surface. Detach and observe. If you still feel very affected and connected to the pain, you may need the next steps to be taken with a therapist. If however you can look objectively at your behavioural pattern you are already letting it go and this in itself will help you to forgive yourself and others thus enabling you to move forward to a more positive response in future. Forgiveness is a huge part of this awareness action so take time to do this in a beneficial manner. Remember if you feel any guilt then you have not forgiven. To accept is to forgive. Be gentle and patient with yourself and see each small step as a step of enlightened soul growth.

This is the biggest gift of love you can give to yourself.

Power Animal

The jaguar resonates with the number five.

Spend time in the harmonious energy of the jaguar. Feel and merge with the flow of this harmonious energy. This will help to bring to your awareness insightful thoughts that help you to understand your own emotional blocks. The energy of the jaguar will help you to detach from your anxieties into a space of harmony.

Harmony is peace. Peace is Source.

SOUL JOURNEY GUIDANCE
SIX

Parent child relationship

Power animal: Swan (Cob and Pen)

Sacred shape: Octahedron

Masters: St Peter and Rosa

Crystal: Desert Rose

The power animal resonating with the vibration of the number six is the swan, both cob and pen — male and female.

The shape that will help us to connect to the vibrational energy of the number six is an octahedron.

The crystal carrying the vibration of St Peter and Rosa and the number six is the desert rose.

The number six carries the eternal wisdom of Source.

The vibration of the number six surrounds the birth of every sentient being; therefore at the birth of every child. We as humans are constantly giving or receiving love and this is done at a deep level through our parent child/child parent relationships.

The vibration of the number six is filled with solutions to one of the hardest challenges that we as material beings experience, which is the parent child/child parent relationship. These relationships are often seen as the strongest relationships in our lives and they will carry with them the solutions to some of the soul growth challenges that are part of that parent child/child parent relationship.

When we tune in and connect to the vibration of six we come to realise that there is always an opposite to everything. If we have brought in a soul growth challenge then we must acknowledge that we will also have a soul growth solution to that challenge. If we have drawn the image with the vibration of the number six then we may need to look more closely at the challenges in our family relationships. Look at the challenges from the detached space of trusting that there is a solution. What is important to understand is that we choose our parents and the surrounding conditions. This is a soul agreement and has been done for the greater evolvement of all concerned. If we can resonate with this it often makes it easier to detach from suffering and pain filled anger that the soul lessons are bringing to us.

Unconditional love is often best learnt in these circumstances. This is why these important relationships can evoke or draw in pure Divine Love that is filled with compassion, empathy, forgiveness and healing.

When this is achieved it can be seen as a family in its fullest Divine potential; however, this is not always the way we perceive or experience our families and the soul growth lessons will often come from taking responsibility in creating a better parent child/child parent relationship.

For many of us this is a huge commitment that needs to come from the Divine within us to be able to take the next steps. The active awareness action below is a small step in starting this process.

Active Awareness Action

Ask yourself about the particular parent child/child parent relationship:
> *What am I afraid of?*
> *How does the relationship make me feel?*
> *Do I feel any guilt?*
> *Am I regarding the challenge in this relationship with a judgemental view?*

Write down your answers as honestly as you can, after all this is for your greater good. Now look at the relationship again as if you are on the outside. With the insights you have received, look at the relationship without guilt. Once you have done this in a way that has no subjective judgement write down what you love most in this relationship. Immerse yourself in the positive feeling that this gives you. Once more look at the relationship from a higher perspective and see what you are learning and receiving from this person (child or parent).

Further Action

Find a quiet space to sit down, take all the answers to the questions you have asked and look at them. Call in St Peter and Rosa or Sananda and visualise yourself in the shape of the octahedron. This shape carries the vibration of the number six. Breathe in, with intention, the octahedron shape of the number six. You are now looking at the relationship you have with your child (or parent) from your highest self, whilst allowing your ego self to speak.

You are allowed to feel anger, disappointment, irritation etc and as you do so you are releasing irrational thoughts and feelings that are not connected to your higher self. In other words you are looking at the situation from a higher perspective, at the same time understanding why your personality self has been so adversely affected. This helps you to find the solution or a tool that you can use to improve the relationship, while at the same time, being more aware of your source self. Be patient, allow the source solutions that the vibration of the number six carries to be unfolded. Solutions will come from understanding and accepting.

Power Animal

The swan resonates with the number six.

Find a peaceful quiet place and call in the energy of this power animal. You will find that you are filled with a quiet strength and wisdom knowing that will help you to communicate with your family from a state of grace in a loving but firm way.

The Divinity within is Grace.

SOUL JOURNEY GUIDANCE
SIX

source energy pattern
ONE + FIVE

Be Mindful of the Present

Being in the state of mindfulness draws in this pattern of one+five of the number six

What is mindfulness?

It is being aware and awake in each moment, being present through the awareness of our surroundings, our body and most importantly our breath. We are not concerned about the past, we are not planning or thinking about the future. We are only concerned with what we are doing in each moment. We are existing in the present moment, free of judgement.

This is when we are the most grounded as we are fully aware of our body and our surroundings. Being grounded in the present moment allows for our full awareness of Source and our source self. We may often hear the expression 'grounded and connected' this is simply being aware of your body and the Life/Source within and without, in any moment.

This is experiencing a state of grace; however for most of us mindfulness can be fleeting, it is an intention that is often inhibited by the mind presenting us with a series of thoughts that we find hard to let go. Like any other technique this needs practice.

What you need to ask yourself is this:

How often am I in a state of mindfulness?

How important is it for me to be mindful of the present moment?

First of all we must not judge our findings, but carry the intention of increasing our mindfulness moments.

One of the best ways to practice mindfulness is through meditation. There are several ways to meditate; through relaxation techniques, breath or mandala focus, mantras, sounds, and many more. It is important to find the correct meditation technique that we resonate with. This will relax our body and then change our brain waves from a beta brain wave (where we function from mostly) to an alpha brain wave state (relaxed walking, listen to soothing music, focused breathing patterns etc) and then the progression if we wish to the theta brain state (here our meditation really starts, we move from the working mind to a deeper relaxed state of awareness.)

From here we will feel disconnected from planning the future or past thoughts and more likely to have visualisations or insights. It is here that we find that the promptings from our source self are more easily understood.

Active Awareness Action

A simple meditation is to relax your physical body by using your breath. The focus on your breath keeps you in the present moment. Find a quiet place where you will not be disturbed, make sure you are sitting or lying comfortably. Do not try to stop thoughts coming in, rather observe them and then let them go.

First take some deep breaths, from the diaphragm, with the intention that you are clearing all anxieties and blockages. Then allow your breath to become a rhythm that feels gentle and comfortable. As you concentrate on how wonderful it is to breathe in source light, breathe this light into each part of your body with the intention that you are filling your body with pure white light of Source.

Start with your feet, go up into the legs, pelvic area, into your trunk filling all your organs, your arms, hands, shoulders, neck and head with the pure white source light. Say to yourself: 'I am pure light, I am the light of Source'. Stay in this perfect space where you are aware of nothing except your source self for as long as it feels right.

When you feel the time is right, bring your attention back into the room, feel yourself sitting comfortably on the chair and when you are ready open your eyes and feel the source light still within you. It is your awareness of your source filled body in this moment that grounds you. Once more focus your mind on your breath and gently wriggle your fingers and toes, feeling full of life.

Power Animal

The swan resonates with the number six.

The swan will help you to find that state of quiet grace, a deep silence where you are free of clutter and can sense that which is beyond ego..

Take time to study the swan's movements and note that the easy gliding is the clutter free part of you and that the fast movements of the swan's feet are the necessary thoughts for forward planning or wise thoughts learnt from past experience which help propel you forward.

Mindfulness is being present.

SOUL JOURNEY GUIDANCE
SIX

source energy pattern
TWO + FOUR

Lessons from Soulmates

Connecting with a soulmate attracts the source energy pattern of two+four.

Soulmate is a term that we often hear when we speak of romantic relationships. We as humans are social beings and from childhood to adulthood a prime need is to love and be loved. It is therefore natural to give and receive love. The purest feeling of source awareness is the feeling of love. This being the case it is not surprising that from a child we look first to our parents for love and as we mature we start looking for love from friends, girlfriends, boyfriends until most of us feel the need to find the 'perfect partner' and it is this perfectly right person that is often referred to as 'a soulmate' or twin flame.

One of the many theories of soulmates is that we belong to a soul group and that a soulmate is part of that soul group. Another is that a soul splits and that we spend this lifetime or others looking for our twin flame or soulmate. You can decide what resonates with you. One thing for sure is that when we meet someone that is part of our soul group, the attraction is immediate. The person will feel familiar to us, and we will feel completely at ease.

The fact that we resonate so profoundly within a short time would indicate that this is a soulmate encounter. We may also feel a wonderful sense of peace and safety. We feel as if we have met our other half. This is because we feel a completeness. Soulmates can be friends, a romantic partner or even a family member. They can be the same gender, opposite gender, the same culture or one from across the world. What is similar is the feeling of wholeness and oneness that fills us when we meet a soulmate.

Being in a soulmate relationship is not always easy and if we have discord or do not like things about ourselves, we will find it hard to understand our soulmate. This can lead to a difficult and disharmonious relationship; however it will lead to a huge soul growth. A soulmate is at their happiest when they accept and love themselves, which in turn is mirrored by the other soulmate.

Sometimes soulmates have put challenges in place that can, on the personality level, be so huge that they can cause a relationship to break down or a friendship to fall apart. A theory is that this would then be worked on in a further lifetime or existence. Soulmates can choose to spend many lifetimes together growing and evolving in huge light steps.

One thing is for certain, if we have a strong desire to meet our soulmate in this lifetime, then we will. The expression 'to fully love another as you fully love yourself' is a part of attracting your soulmate. However remember that we may have more than one soulmate as our soul may have put in place unfinished lessons or karma that needs understanding and forgiveness. These are soul level decisions and choices that we knew about before we came to Earth. This would have been part of the soul contract for this particular lifetime and part of the essence of Conscious awakening in our continuing soul journey.

Active Awareness Action

Call on the masters St Peter, Rosa and Sananda to surround you in their loving light. It is the gratitude you feel for your connection to Source that fills you with love.

Find a quiet place that fills you with gratitude, your garden, out in the woods or a favourite part of your home. This gratitude will help lift your vibrational energy. Think about everything you like about yourself. This is an indication of what you would attract in your soul mate, your joyous self.

Now think about your challenging aspects and study them, accept them. Acknowledge how these aspects have taken you to situations where you have learnt the most about yourself.

Remember that your soulmate will also have similar traits; however you will find that having faced these challenging traits in yourself you will respond with empathy and understanding. This will attract a similar response from your soulmate.

This will lead to wonderful, fulfilling, heart touching, heart relationships, especially in a romantic soulmate relationship.

You will feel blessed. Others will see you as blessed.

Power Animal

The swan resonates with the number six.

The swan holds, and is in touch with, the wisdom of the universe; both the cob and the pen hold huge compassion for human life. They have a full understanding of those aspects of us we do not want to admit to, aspects we deny. Allow the compassionate wisdom of this power animal to fill you with the courage to face all aspects of yourself and thus allow the soul desire to share your life with a soulmate become a reality. Love yourself fully and in turn you will love the other that is part of your soul.

To love is to give and receive in equal amounts.

SOUL JOURNEY GUIDANCE
SIX

source energy pattern
THREE + THREE

Accept and Move Forward

When we surrender we attract the source energy pattern of three+three.

The vibration of the number six is around birth (beginning of a time) and death (end of a time). This is applicable for all life as well as the material forms we have created. An example would be a painting or sculpture that we have put our life force into and it is then broken or destroyed.

The Source in us creates for a reason, an expression, a need to experience. It also expresses itself in our creations. Our creations can be books, paintings, food, gardens, craft of any kind. This can also be singing, poetry, prose, and even heartfelt presentations. Every expression that is filled with joy and contentment, that engenders a feeling of contentment, is our extension of Source. All creation in this linear timeline has a beginning and an end. It is the acceptance of this reality that allows us to move forward.

Sometimes we face a challenge in our lives that creates a huge resistance. An example would be, we lose the job of a lifetime or we do not succeed in passing a life changing exam. We cannot accept this. We make excuses or look to blame someone else or something else. We cannot face the reality of what has happened and we start distancing ourselves from our source self. We refuse to accept and so we cannot move forward. This is denying that we are Source and that everything is an experience and expression of Source.

One of the biggest challenges that we as humans all face at some point is the feeling of grief. This is often at the passing of a person or animal that has been close to us. This will always draw the number six in the pattern of three+three. This is what helps us to accept. Grief can be devastating and we may come to a standstill through the emotion of grief. This is one of the hardest lessons brought to us in our three dimensional reality that experiences linear time.

Active Awareness Action

Grief is just one aspect of resistance, which can also be experienced as anger, denial, depression, lethargy or a disinterest in life. We can overcome this resistance by living each day in the moment, taking small steps of trust and surrender to a state of acceptance and allowing our source self to take over.

At this time in your life you may feel the need to ask for help from friends, family, therapists or counsellors, whoever you feel drawn to.

However if you choose to help yourself you can call on the light of Source. This will help you to surrender to the reality of 'all that is'.

If you feel you need help and guidance from a professional do not ignore this as you will be responding to your higher source self and will be guided to the right vibrational energy. This movement in itself is the first step to acceptance and moving forward.

It is through the act of acceptance that the pattern of three+three is at its strongest. This, in turn, helps us to take small steps towards recovery and thus move forward in our lives.

To accept is to surrender to what is, to accept the reality that has been created. This is when healing starts through the growing awareness of our source self. If we accept the reality of 'what is' in our lives, we can move our life forward in a completely different way. This can be a soul evolvement of huge proportions. Acceptance is not about 'making your bed and having to lie on it' it is about accepting the reality of 'what is' in this moment. This absolute connection to Source then enables us to make choices and move on.

Further action

Place Divine Love in the shape of an etheric octahedron around you. Use your source filled breath and the power of intent to do this. This healing vibration will help you to accept and move forward.

Power Animal

The swan resonates with the number six.

The swan, like all power animals is a true example of source acceptance and moving forward from that space. *Feel yourself surrounded by the energy of the swan. Allow this power animal to help you raise your vibration enough to be connected to your own wisdom.*

We are all wise beings. When we own our own wisdom we can take comfort that we are never alone at an energetic level.

View reality from our source self and take a step forward.

SOUL JOURNEY GUIDANCE
SEVEN

Attention to the breath

Power animal:	Dolphin
Sacred shape:	The Seed of Life – Seven Interlocking Spheres
Masters:	John the Baptist or Saint Germain
Crystals:	Blue Lace Agate or Amethyst

The power animal resonating with the vibration of the number seven is the dolphin

The sacred shape that will help us to connect to the vibrational energy of the number seven is the 'seed of life'.

The crystals that carries the vibration of John the Baptist or Saint Germain and the number seven are blue lace agate and amethyst.

The number seven is an extraordinary number; it has a powerful vibration that has been recognised by religions and cultures through the ages. So why are we so drawn to the vibration of the number seven? It is the bridge between the material world and consciousness. It is the dimensional bridge between what is and what can be.

Our breath carries the vibration of the number seven. We as humans need air to live and whether we breathe air to live or live to breathe source filled air, we are bridging that space between our material being and our source light being. Pure air is a source filled gift from the minute we first draw breath. We are potential 'masters of breath' and, if we allow it, we can choose to change our lives and our days through how we use and understand breath. We can use our breath to bring us to consciousness awareness. In our pure Source Consciousness, we become the bridge of light between material form and Source, God, the Divine, whichever term we resonate with. Another way of understanding this is to see that each source filled breath carries infinite possibilities and that each time we breathe we are accessing the gateway to all that is.

How do we access the gateway to the understanding of 'all that is'? We can do this through 'source conscious breathing'. There are many methods of source conscious breathing; however the simplest is finding your own rhythm of breath that is perfectly right for you. Once you feel in harmony with your breath, allow yourself to enjoy the sound of your breath, the feel of your breath. All the time you do this, your awareness through being in the moment, in the present through your attention to your breath, is the most powerful act you can focus on in your day.

This is Source Conscious Breath.

Healing with your breath

The vibration of the number seven is strong around any desire to heal our body through breath conscious awareness. First understand it is the conscious awareness that we are beings of light that instigates the healing process. Thus using our breath is a way to focus our attention to achieve this awareness.

Active Awareness Action

Settle yourself and close your eyes. With each soft breath feel yourself relax, let go of all stress, all judgement, listen to your heartbeat, the life in you. Now listen to your breath, hear your breath, your own rhythm of breath, feel how your body surrenders to a place of peace, let your body respond in a softening manner; you are 'no body' just energy; you have no stress, you are just space, stillness. From this space take seven deep breaths, using your diaphragm.

With each in breath feel yourself becoming filled with source light, with each out breath breathe out blocks to your healing process. Now allow your mind to feel yourself in good health; how wonderful you would feel. This is the feeling that lifts your vibration. Feel well, feel whole. Breathe that feeling of wellness into your cells, your organs and your entire body. Using your own source rhythm breath, breathe in wellness and breathe out your gratitude for this happening. Do this as often as you can. Each time you capture that feeling of wellbeing you are making the possibility of wellbeing a reality. John the Baptist and Saint Germain will help you to stay with the feeling of being blessed.

Further Action

You can choose to use the sacred shape of 'the seed of life'. This is a powerful way to access the vibration of seven. Using source breath and powerful intent, breathe this shape around you.

When you are fully connected to this sacred shape, call in source energy with your breath and with intention breathe this energy around you, and let the breath of life within the 'seed of life' help you to see a blessing in each part of your day. Each blessing can grow into an opportunity to experience life in a more fulfilling way. It is your gratitude for all of your blessings that waters and feeds these blessings with love and light and expands the joy and bliss in your life.

Power Animal

The dolphin resonates with the number seven.

The dolphin has long been associated with helping humans in the healing process. See yourself in the water with dolphins around you, feel uplifted and how your stress and worries melt away. They will help you to live in the moment, to experience the freedom of being present in the most joyful manner. Capture this feeling and breathe it into your body, sense how much better you feel. Let this feeling become a joyful signature that you can experience any time. Use your Source Conscious breath to breathe this in.

Become a master of Source Conscious Breath.

SOUL JOURNEY GUIDANCE
SEVEN

source energy pattern
ONE + SIX

Water's Healing Powers

The pattern of one+six is always drawn to us as we awaken to the life force in water. The truth of water and the hidden wisdom in each droplet and molecule of water vibrates with the pattern of the number seven. We can change our lives once we become masters of living water. This means we understand that water is Source and that it carries all possibilities. However, this in turn carries the responsibility of how we treat our water.

Do you see water as a blessing?

Do you bless the water with your gratitude each time you use it?

Do you notice water that is dis-eased? Do you help to bring it back to harmony?

This can be done energetically or even physically. An energetic example is sending love and light into the water. A physical example is not to put anything that is toxic into the water.

Water helps us to heal through purifying us energetically. This is done through intention and gratitude, standing in the rain, lying in a bath of water, showering or swimming in the sea. It is our pleasure, gratitude and intention to purify that draws in this pattern seven and intensifies the purification. Water is life, and life is in the water within us; each molecule of water within us carries the truth of Source. The healing possibilities of Source are within each molecule and atom of water in our body.

We can, through Source Consciousness, become masters in changing the atoms and molecules of water through intention from the space of being conscious in each moment. *If you have been drawn to this image then look at your relationship with water. How do you see water? Are you aware that your material body is mainly made up of water? (approximately 70%).*

Do you drink enough water?

Active Awareness Action

If you are drawn to the energy of John the Baptist or Saint Germain then call in his blessing and feel his pure white light fill every molecule of water in your body. Use your breath and breathe in the source light with the intention of healing the water in your body.

Start from your feet and breathe in the healing light and the vibration of the pattern one+six of the number seven into each atom of water; feel how, as the molecules of water in your body are restructured to be 'Source structured molecules', you tingle with the force of life.

Move your attention to your legs, trunk, chest, arms and hands, all the time focusing on the water molecules being restructured and bringing balance and harmony into your body. Continue to move up your body to your shoulders, neck, face and the whole of your head. Your body will vibrate with source energy. See the pure source structured water healing all dis-ease in your body.

Take your focus and intention to any area of your body that you feel needs healing. Listen to the life force in your body; you may feel areas of your body responding to the healing by going hot or cold, tingling or even throbbing. Just surrender to the healing Source within and trust that your source self is bringing balance and harmony to your body. This is something you can do in a meditation or while bathing or swimming. Wherever feels right for you.

Further Action

Here are some ideas to use the water in your life to its fullest potential.

Consider the water that you drink: Bless your water with heartfelt gratitude for all that it does for you. Intend that the water has everything in it that you need for a day filled with wellbeing. Where possible drink your water at room temperature. If your water comes from a tap allow it to rest before drinking, while resting the water will start correcting itself.

You can use the water as the base for a tincture carrying the memories of the properties of any plants that you have been drawn to use. Whenever you serve water to a guest/client take steps to give them the highest vibrational water possible infused with love for them in the knowledge that we are all one.

Power Animal

The dolphin resonates with the number seven.

Some are blessed to actually swim with the dolphins; however you can call on the dolphins to surround you in their energy and then surrender to the joy of seeing and feeling yourself swimming with these ancient beings of wisdom.

Dolphins carry the spiritual wisdom of lifetimes of evolvement and healing is as natural to them as breathing or swimming.

Water carries the memory of who we are.

SOUL JOURNEY GUIDANCE
SEVEN

source energy pattern
TWO + FIVE

We are all healers

Energy healing is a projection of unconditional love. It is the loving intention of our source selves to help or heal others. All healing modalities carry the vibration of the number seven but when it is through the strong intention of our awakening source selves to heal through unconditional love it carries the pattern of two+five of the number seven.

Unconditional love carries the highest Source vibration; it is the vibration of the Divine Mother. Unconditional love carries compassion and is quite free of judgement. It becomes limitless source healing. Consider how a mother holds her hurt child and pours compassion and love into her child. She is healing because her intention is for the well being of her child. This draws in the pattern of two+five in a powerful way.

We are all able to heal through unconditional love. We may be drawn to go into a healing service for others as a career; it will be part of our own soul journey of enlightenment. It is important to remember that our life journey involves being aware of what needs to be healed in ourselves, in order to move from the feeling of separateness and become one with the cosmos. This is why we are here. This is why we are often drawn to clients/others who have had similar challenges of pain or suffering. If we recognise this it allows us to become an observer of our own healing needs. It also allows us to work with heartfelt compassion and empathy towards another.

When we are drawn to the welfare of others, we will draw the vibration of the number seven towards us. One of the strongest pulls on this particular source energy pattern is when caring is a principle factor within a family dynamic; this is very often a soul decision and the two+five pattern will be part of the energetic signature of each of the people involved.

This source energy pattern of the number seven allows us to be guided to the correct energy healing modality. There are many energy healing modalities, more so now than ever before and it may feel confusing. This is when calling in the vibration of the number seven will help us to recognise and know which is the perfect healing vibration for us.

As we grow spiritually our vibration changes and we may find that, after using or even teaching one or more healing modalities, we are still searching and feel drawn to other healing vibrations. This will be part of our soul journey. Embrace this growth and give thanks for what we have learnt previously, then step forward with an acceptance and gratitude for the next part of our service to others.

Active Awareness Action

One of the best ways to embrace a healing service career choice is to have as high a vibration as possible. There are many ways to lift your vibration. If you feel drawn to this image then call for the purifying energy of Source to surround you; ask for a blessing of source light, drink it in, breathe it in, feel yourself being flooded and filled with this purifying white light. John the Baptist and Saint Germain will be helping and supporting you. Feel yourself blessed. From this feeling, think about your choices. You will find that you are filled with clarity and deep knowing of what fills your heart with joy.

This is your source self communicating with you.

Further action

You may be drawn to sit in the sacred shape of the seed of life filled with the vibration of the number seven. This shape carries all the seeds of possible choices that are perfect for you. Do not rush this. Take time each day to be in this space of possibilities and you will attract whatever it is that you need.

Think of how you would feel if you were in healing service to others.

Does it feel like joy? Or perhaps a peaceful contentment?

Breathe this feeling into your body. From this feeling, experience its wonder; from this space you will find it easier to be aware of your source self. Try to spend as much time in this state of awareness and feel how strongly your source self prompts you in the right direction.

Power Animal

The dolphin resonates with the number seven.

If you are drawn to the dolphin, then you will respond strongly to its energy of fun, the joy it expresses in the sounds it makes, in its exuberance of movement, in its loving commitment to other dolphins. All of this will raise your vibration and fill you with the awareness of what is right for you.

There is joy in everything we do.

SOUL JOURNEY GUIDANCE
SEVEN

source energy pattern
THREE + FOUR

Awaken your Passion for Life

A passion for life is movement towards spiritual awakening. When we desire happiness and wellbeing in our life, this desire, this passion, draws in the pattern three+four of the number seven.

The need and desire to be happy is in all of us. Happiness is different for each of us. To one it may be to wonder at the beauty of a rose, to another it may be to walk along a beach, to create a picture, listen to bird song, or even swim with dolphins.

Endless lists can be written about what happiness means to different people. What is common to all is that in these moments of experiencing happiness, we are in the heart of the moment, we are in connection with our divine loving source self, experiencing Source through this high vibrational emotion that we call happiness. From these moments of happiness comes a creative joyful desire to be more, create more, to become more than we think we are. Recognise this as an awakening to the abundance in source self.

As we awaken to the bliss within, the material wants and needs in our life become less important and there ignites within us a burning desire to become whole, to be reunited with our source self. This becomes the focus of our desires. The beautiful universal paradox is, that as we become more focused on our growing awareness, we effortlessly attract what we need in the material world.

We will discover that we are limitless in our source selves, and it is the desire or passion that we feel towards different ideas, hopes and dreams that ignites the will of Source within.

Healing with Passion

If we desire health 'with all our heart' this passion or desire is a powerful intention. The vibration of the number seven is in the intention to heal; however, it is the passion and strong desire, like a burning light coursing through us, that draws the pattern of three+four.

Why is that so powerful?

To feel passionate about something holds the element of fire. This consuming powerful vibration helps us to keep our focus on the desired outcome and so create our reality in a powerful way.

Our personality selves are constantly being prompted by our source selves; however, it is the passion of Source that is Divine Love and Divine Will that makes a possibility into a fulfilling reality.

Passion, or the creative fire within, can also be used in a way that is not always for our highest good. We are creators; however, if we are manipulated by our ego personality self the passion within may become all consuming fear and destroy and create chaos mentally, emotionally, spiritually and physically. This will be used by our source self as a soul growth opportunity; however, our life journey may be a difficult one.

It may be that you need to examine what you are passionate about in your life.

Active Awareness Action

The sacred shape of the seed of life is the perfect source shape to call around us when we are awakening to all that we are.

Feel the safe, strong energy of this shape around you. Breathe in the Source vibration of seven. Remember that the number seven carries the vibration of healing on all levels, physically, emotionally, mentally and spiritually

Take time to consider what you desire most in your life, sense how passionate you feel about it. Now spend time focusing on how you would feel if your desire was a reality. Allow yourself to feel gratitude for what you will receive. As you sit in this space of gratitude for your desired outcome, trust and surrender to this outcome. Have you noticed that when you feel passionate about something or consumed with a desire to make it happen that nothing or nobody can sway you? This is when healing happens, when dreams and hopes become reality. This is the source self in you making the possibility you desire a fulfilling reality.

Power Animal

The dolphin resonates with the number seven.

If you are drawn to the dolphin this will help you to find the passion within. To be passionate is to focus with an all consuming intention. This means that you need to be in the present moment, not allowing past beliefs or future worries to cloud your focus. The strength of focus that the dolphins hold will help you with your focus and intention. Breathe in the energy of the dolphins and allow their wisdom to help you to commit passionately to what is perfectly right for you.

Passion for life is the essence of Source.

SOUL JOURNEY GUIDANCE
EIGHT

Facing Life Changes
What needs changing in your life at this time?

Power animals:	Tiger & Red Admiral Butterfly
Sacred shape:	Star Tetrahedron
Master:	Moses
Crystal:	Red Jasper

The power animals resonating with the vibration of the number eight are the tiger and the red admiral butterfly

The source energy shape that will help us to connect to the vibrational energy of the number eight is a star tetrahedron.

The crystal that carries the vibration of the master Moses and the number eight is red jasper.

Soul Journey Number Eight

We are eternal, experiencing a temporary existence. We are eternal beings of light in a three dimensional linear time phase. Our life here reflects this, in that it is made up of a series of phases, some running concurrently. An example would be 'being in a relationship, being a parent, being at work, being retired, being ill, being educated, being poor' etc.

When we draw the vibration of the number eight towards us it is because we are being prompted by our source selves to either move to the next phase or to modify a particular phase so that it is more in alignment with our divine will. *You will always find the vibration of eight is drawn to you when you are making empowering changes in your life.*

One of the best ways to do this is to ask yourself these questions:

> *Am I happy with all aspects of my life?*
> *Do I long for this time or phase in my life to change or even end?*
> *Do I feel afraid to end a certain phase?*
> *Are the consequences of changing a phase or aspect of my life prohibiting me from making a decision?*

When you have answered these questions honestly, allow yourself to contemplate the idea that you can change or modify this particular phase for your greater welfare and happiness.

> *Does this worry me?*   *Do I feel unsettled?*
> *Do I feel a sense of freedom, liberation even?*
> *Am I excited by the thought of change?*

Bear in mind that feeling unsettled may be your unconscious mind prompting you to beware of change. 'Nothing is forever' can mean that everything material has a linear timeline that has a beginning and an end.

Now look at the same phrase from a different perspective. If we say No Thing (meaning the 'true' us is not material) *is forever* (meaning eternal) we are saying that we are eternal Source. This is why our limiting beliefs can be altered.

We can change if we choose to. This is free will. Free will is about listening to our inner voice without being affected by old beliefs and thought patterns, habits and behaviours and cultural or religious structures that no longer serve our higher good. We can change a phase, we can moderate a phase, we can even end certain phases in our lives. Change can, as a soul growth experience, enable us to move forward on our life journey.

Active Awareness Action

Sometimes making a change means overcoming a fear. This can be traced back to childhood. Some believe that past lives can affect us. We may even have inherited ancestral fears. It may be appropriate at this stage to seek a therapist for advice.

To be able to face the cause of your fear in a detached manner you need to be in a place of mindfulness. This in turn will help you to have greater clarity and understanding of the cause of your fears and consequent blocks. This understanding will enable the process of change. This will take fortitude and strong determination: Moses will help you. The best way to do this is through regular meditation, if you can be determined and disciplined enough to put a fifteen to thirty minute time slot aside for yourself each day you will find that staying in a place of mindfulness throughout the rest of the day becomes easier.

Further Action

To help with this use the shape, the star tetrahedron. See or imagine yourself surrounded by this shape. Sit quietly in this energetic space and feel the confusion and blocks becoming signposts to help you understand what you do not want in order to understand clearly what you do want.

You will find that the harmonising vibration of this sacred shape will help you to engage in a quiet introspection of your thoughts and emotions enabling you to recognise habitual fear based thoughts that are often attached to past uncomfortable or even traumatic memories. The more you work within this sacred shape the more you will detach from fear. Greater possibilities and changes will become accessible in your life.

Power Animal

The tiger resonates with the number eight. *Call for this magnificent power animal to help you to find the courage to make a stand where it is needed. Perhaps you need stronger boundaries in the different areas in your life. Feel yourself become the tiger, feel how strong and fearless you are. How does this make you feel? Keep this empowering feeling with you as you make these life altering changes.*

All changes signify an opportunity for soul growth.

SOUL JOURNEY GUIDANCE
EIGHT

source energy pattern
ONE + SEVEN

Resistance to Change

When we are drawn to this pattern one+seven of the number eight, it will mean that we have come to a crossroads in our life and a choice is required. The vibration of eight is always around us when it is time for us to acknowledge our mastery. This means we have to own our decisions and take responsibility for the changes that we create.

When we reach a crossroads on our life pathway we are never alone, we will find our guides are close, our ability to connect to our higher self or source self is made easier through this pattern vibration. The synchronicity in finding the right spiritual helpers, books, etc often plays a part in this. This crossroads in our life becomes a soul enlightenment window.

Our spiritual awareness expands from the decisions and choices we make, the insights we receive and the deepening of our understanding. What we need to understand is that from a soul perspective there is no wrong choice, just a different timeline of events that bring different challenges and blocks that ultimately bring us to the awareness that we are Source, here to experience duality in a linear timeline with the ultimate goal of becoming one with Source.

Knowing this, why do we sometimes feel a resistance to change? One reason is that we become so immersed in our physical lives, where we often face day to day issues in a place of stress and worry, that when we face a decision it can come from a thought pattern of anxiety, therefore there is no clarity, only a sense of panic in the decision making.

A further reason is that from childhood many of us are conditioned to respond in a certain way to an outside occurrence. This is a subconscious reaction each time a similar stimulus occurs. An example would be if we had to move house as a child and our parents were hugely stressed by this, to the extent that it subsequently affected us in a painful way. We could associate moving home with that stress.

Each time we think of moving home, even if it would ultimately be a wise family decision, that same painful feeling would be resurrected by our subconscious minds resulting in a resistance to that particular change. This is why resistance to change needs to be examined from a higher perspective, our source selves. We need to be in a space where we are in our creative conscious mind, bringing us into the present. We need to stay in that space for as long as possible.

Active Awareness Action

One way to do this is to meditate, by sitting somewhere quietly and concentrating on your breathing which helps you to stay present.

When you are facing resistance in life it will sometimes be difficult to relax into a meditation so take time to place yourself in a secluded place where you are undisturbed and allow the time you need to find that quiet space within, where you can allow your thoughts to gently float in; however, do not attach to them only observe. Now you can face your resistance as an observer.

Alternatively you could go for a walk in nature where you become fully aware of your surroundings. From your place of peace and awareness take time to face your resistance to change.

If you feel drawn to the master Moses, call for his help to strengthen your focus in being present. Surround yourself with his energy by saying his name and feeling grateful for his help.

Further Action

Surround yourself with the sacred shape the star tetrahedron, this will help you to strengthen your focus in being present and in harmony with your source self. Do this whenever you have time to yourself in the day, whether it is ten minutes or much longer, stay present and see the resistance from the awareness of your higher self. See the resistance as a thought form followed by an emotion, which is not the reality, this will help you to detach from the resistance and see your life crossroads with clarity and free from fear. Keep in mind that you can use the star tetrahedron during a mindful meditation or a meditative walk.

Power Animal

The tiger resonates with the number eight.

This dynamic power animal can help you to stay in the present. Become the tiger, be aware of your surroundings, be aware of your senses, what you see, what you hear, what you can smell, even feel your breath through your body. Take a walk in nature feeling yourself aware of the slightest sounds, the song of the birds, the rustling of leaves. All this will heighten your senses, keeping you in the present moment.

Freedom from resistance allows us to make a source aligned choice.

SOUL JOURNEY GUIDANCE
EIGHT

source energy pattern
TWO + SIX

Moving beyond Grief

Experiencing grief, sorrow or heartache in our life journey comes to most of us. Whether it is the passing of a loved one, a beloved pet or the ending of a romantic relationship or marriage, it is still ending a phase in our lives. Grief can have a severe traumatic effect on us, bringing about the feeling of lack, which is a natural emotional outcome from loss. It is also a very personal journey and we all experience this loss in different degrees.

However grief attracts the vibrational pattern two+six of the number eight towards us, which in turn will attract the correct assistance in the way of grief counselling, friends and family who support us, help books, videos and much more. It is our choice to discern which we need.

A common challenge is feeling alone at the loss of a partner. This often happens in long term relationships and the perception is that the feeling of loneliness may not change in the future. For some it feels as if a part of them is missing and the expression 'broken hearted' is exceedingly apt. Many couples have spent a lifetime together and so with the physical loss comes the emotional fear of not knowing how to continue without the partner's support. There is also the fear of being alone in a space that has always known company.

Another challenge is if our grief is surrounded by guilt. For example, if a loved one was ill and we did not visit or help as much as we had intended. There are many types of guilt around loss of any kind. This needs to be looked at in a consciously aware manner in order to move away from guilt and towards acceptance. This can take time and needs the understanding and support from those who are close to us.

Grief affects in different degrees and sometimes it is hard to accept another's indifference or lack of emotional support. This can often happen within family environments. The feeling of loss then becomes mixed with emotions of anger, resentment and suppression.

This is a time when this vibrational energy pattern will help us to discover the strength within and the courage to express ourselves in a way that will help those unaware family members to understand more fully.

One way to move forward is to acknowledge that we are allowed to process the grief of our loss in a way that is right for us as an individual. There will inevitably be change in our lives, some things may be as good as or even better in some ways, but different. This is a step to acceptance and moving forward.

Grief can come in stages and waves of emotion. This can be debilitating and a time when it is good to talk to those who have empathy towards us. This may be a time when a process of grief counselling is needed.

Grief can make us feel powerless and the journey towards acceptance and wholeness, which may include blame, anger, guilt and hopelessness is a process from which we can grow and change. It can even be a catalyst towards something inspirational that we never expected.

We can also experience grief for the ending of a work phase or career. Even retirement can bring the emotional feeling of loss. All of these situations carry loss and therefore invoke feelings of emptiness and lack. From here it is the journey back to wholeness and completeness that holds soul growth.

Active Awareness Action

Use the sacred shape of the star tetrahedron, which will help you to cope with the loss. Allow yourself to accept the help from the pattern two+six through acknowledging that you are complete while experiencing the present; you are your source self. This knowing is a powerful part of the healing process. The master Moses together with Sananda and Mary will help you cope with loss.

The energy of the star tetrahedron is especially powerful when you need to forgive yourself or forgive others. Place yourself into an etheric star tetrahedron. Using your breath, breathe the light of Source into this sacred geometric shape. Do this as often as you need.

Power Animal

The tiger and the red admiral butterfly resonate with the number eight.

Call for the energy of the tiger to surround you in its constancy. This power animal will have direct and to the point answers that may surprise you, but help you to understand and overcome the trauma that grief can bring. This enables you to accept and move forward.

Alternatively, the red admiral butterfly will help you to come to terms with changes in your life.

Acceptance is the catalyst for change.

SOUL JOURNEY GUIDANCE
EIGHT

source energy pattern
THREE + FIVE

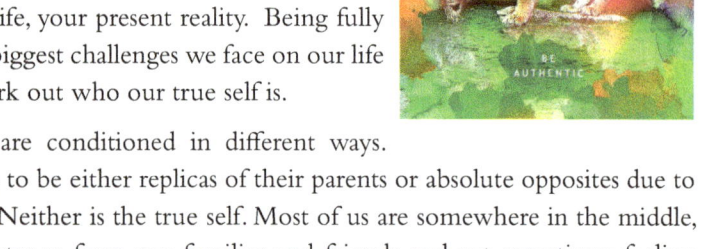

Be Authentic

Number eight is about claiming your own mastery, your ability to change your life, your present reality. Being fully authentic is one of the biggest challenges we face on our life journey. We have to work out who our true self is.

From a child we are conditioned in different ways. Some children grow up to be either replicas of their parents or absolute opposites due to a feeling of rebellion. Neither is the true self. Most of us are somewhere in the middle, wanting love and acceptance from our families and friends and yet sometimes feeling trapped or resentful over certain things we do or even feel we have to do.

If you have drawn this image and pattern three+five of the number eight then it is time to look for the true you and what you need and desire in your life.

We can be so conditioned with these thought patterns, that we feel this is the truth of who we are. However, if we are not really happy and feel unsettled and at times sad or even angry then this is an indication that we are not in a place of authenticity. If we feel like this we will be drawing in the powerful pattern of three+five of the number eight to help us find our true self, our authentic self.

It is essential that we do this, because if we are not our true selves we are not in alignment to our source self and service to Source. If we are not sure of our own boundaries we cannot be truly authentic in our dealings with others, as it is impossible to place healthy boundaries for interaction with others.

When we are not living as our authentic selves, we will find our boundaries are not in line with our needs. This causes confusion in others as well as making us unsure of what we want and can create depression and other mental dis-ease.

An example: If a child grows up being told that certain behaviours are not suitable for them, or perhaps high performance is expected of them, this will often create anxiety. The child will then try to conform, to please their parents, often ignoring his or her own needs.

This leads the growing child to learn a pattern of behaviour and habits that receive accolades and praise. The problem arises when, as an adult, we are still trying to conform to others' expectations. This can be partners, workplace colleagues or friends.

This creates an uneasy, unfulfilled life and an inability to connect with others with true authenticity.

Please note that this is in varying degrees and it is important to look at your life and simply ask these questions:

Am I doing what I want to do?

Do I feel content?

Whenever the intent is to be authentic and to face our fears with honesty and courage, we draw this vibration towards us.

Active Awareness Action

These questions are best answered when you are consciously in the present moment through either meditation, or keeping yourself focused, whilst being completely honest. This can be hard, because being honest is relative to what you feel in the moment.

What if you allowed yourself to surrender to these questions by imagining that you are your higher self and asking your personality self in a detached but loving way? This is when you often get an unexpected answer.

You can choose to call on the energy of the master Moses and the star tetrahedron to help you to look at the answers you receive, free from resistance. These resistance free answers are the steps towards you finding your authentic self, your source self.

Power Animal

The tiger and the red admiral butterfly resonate with the number eight.

Call on the tiger to help you to be your authentic self, to be free from inhibiting fears that stop you from being your true self. Ask this powerful animal to walk by your side whenever you have to interact, in an authentic way, with others. You need to act and speak with integrity in order for you to evolve. See yourself stepping into mastery in all walks of life and being your true authentic self, your source self.

Alternatively, see yourself as this beautiful butterfly flying free from worry or uncertain boundaries, you know exactly where to fly and where to land. Allow yourself to have the freedom from your own fearful boundaries to 'fly' to boundaries that are perfectly in line with your authentic source self.

Our authentic self is our source self

SOUL JOURNEY GUIDANCE
EIGHT

source energy pattern
FOUR + FOUR

Receiving What You Create

We are in control of our lives and we choose whether to be a victim or not. This is cause and effect. The 'cause' can be seen as the thoughts, habits and actions, and the 'effect' can be seen as the circumstances and relating conditions.

We may be in a place where we are unhappy with our lives as we see the same situations reoccur and the same problems in relationships, our finances and careers. At this time we are all in the process of claiming our mastery and with that in mind we need to consider the consequences of our thoughts, choices, habits and actions (causes) and subsequent situations (effects). This expression is a law of the Universe, and is heard in many different ways; *'We get what we give.' 'We reap what we sow.'*

These have the underlining message that we create 'a cause' which attracts 'an effect', a happening or situation in our future lives. In the past the effect could be felt years or even lifetimes later. This is called karma.

However, as we are in an age of transition it seems as if the effect is now almost immediate. This is seen more and more in our present lives. It is true that some of us have traumatic and debilitating circumstances; however, it is how we face and respond to these conditions, (poverty, sickness, stress) that makes us a victim or a master of our lives.

It is easy to blame others and believe that nothing can change. When we believe we are victims, which is an exhausting and painful place, we can change our circumstances by modifying our thought patterns and habitual actions.

We can change this by stepping into our mastery and examining those thoughts from a place, our source self, that is free from fear. This in turn enables us to take control of our lives by creating new realities through different positive uplifting thoughts. This is a huge commitment and can be life changing; however it takes practice and mental fortitude to have a constant awareness of what our thoughts are and the resultant emotions from those habitual thoughts.

Active Awareness Action

There are many different ideas and avenues of help that are available to achieve control of your life; however, you need to first commit to the idea that you can change the cause and thus the effect. In other words, you are causing the effect.

The energy of the sacred shape of the star tetrahedron will help you to commit to this attitude of empowerment, the master Moses will also help.

When you start taking responsibility for your responses or reactions to your circumstances and intend to master any thoughts that are not part of your higher self, but fearful ego personality projections, you will draw the pattern four+four towards you which will help you to fortify your intentions.

One of the strongest ways to watch your thoughts and actions is to stay in the present moment as much as you can, enabling you to be more aware of your source self.

When you find yourself thinking a fearful thought you will find it easier to detach and understand why you have that particular thought pattern. Once you understand why you are thinking these victim thoughts, you will be able to move forward towards uplifting and empowering thoughts and actions.

Further Action

Surround and immerse yourself in the energy of the star tetrahedron. Focus on your source filled breath while feeling the gratitude and love filling you in the acknowledgement that you are Source. Practise this daily. This will help you to focus only on positive thoughts throughout your day.

Power Animal

The tiger and the red admiral butterfly resonate with the number eight.

Ask to walk by the side of the tiger and allow your thoughts to merge with this amazing being. See how many of your thoughts are personality self fear based and not necessary for your greater happiness or wellbeing.

This will help you in your everyday life to consider the habitual thoughts that bring lack and unhappiness, and in turn, the thoughts that draw your source self to you. Become an observer with the help of the tiger. This will help you to have an impartial, free from judgement, attitude. Alternatively, allow this being to show you how you can be free of all fear based constraints by being completely in the present. Or perhaps you prefer to imagine that you have the wings of a butterfly you can fly wherever you want. The past perceived difficulties are seen from a greater height, which enables you to see the bigger picture. There may be things you have not noticed before which will change how you respond to the situation.

Now allow your wings to take you beyond your limitations and to places you did not dare to go to before. This will allow your thoughts to expand, emotions that you have buried to express themselves, this will help to show what you have hidden from yourself.

Facing these thoughts and emotions takes you away from being a victim. You can start to choose your thoughts and in doing so master your emotions.

Freedom comes from overcoming thoughts of fear.

SOUL JOURNEY GUIDANCE
NINE

Find your Core Purpose

the core purpose to your existence

Power animals:	White Husky and the Hare
Sacred shape:	Octahedron surrounded by a Sphere
Masters:	Mary Magdalena or Tara
Crystals:	Labradorite or Moonstone

The power animals resonating with the vibration of the number nine are the white husky and the hare.

The shape that will help us to connect to the vibrational energy of the number nine is an octahedron surrounded by a sphere.

The crystals that carry the vibration of Mary Magdalena or Tara and the number nine is labradorite and moonstone.

Soul Journey Number Nine

As we become awakened we evolve to a greater awareness of our source self also known as our higher self, the part of us that is 'all that is': the creator in us.

We are creations of the creator that can in turn create

A question that arises in many of us when we awaken to our source self is:

What is my soul purpose?
What is my core purpose?

It may take many years of self understanding and development to understand the core purpose of our life on Earth. This is an evolving journey.

When we are first aware of our spiritual self we are all in touch with the need to serve. This is a powerful expression of Source and we may rush out enthusiastically to find something that we deem to be spiritual to learn it and pass it on. This can often be disappointing or unfulfilling as we do not feel as happy and content as we feel we should. This is perhaps because we are only building a foundation to what we will be doing and the unsettled feeling is making us aware that we need to look further. However, everything is as it is meant to be and there will be a reason why we were originally guided to that place, or person. The lesson here is to be able to move on with gratitude and no regrets. One of the ways to help us to find our core purpose is to spend time thinking of what we do not want; that which affects us in a negative way. Once we have looked at what we do not want, we can allow ourselves to contemplate that to which we are drawn. The clear picture of what we do not want will enable us to have a clear understanding of what brings us peace, contentment and happiness

This is a step towards knowing our soul or core purpose. Equally, it must be understood that limiting thoughts and emotions will hinder any source promptings that we receive and this will prolong the time it takes for us to awaken fully to our soul purpose. However, it will just mean that more lessons will be learnt on a different pathway that will still take us to the awareness of our soul purpose.

An example of this would be: if we struggle with speaking to a large group, it would be easy to feel that our core purpose could not possibly include public speaking. There is a danger of limiting our potential and ourselves. It is possible to overcome this struggle. Once the struggle has been overcome it demonstrates that our limiting beliefs do not stop us from achieving our soul purpose, just that we may need to take a roundabout route that may involve other insightful challenges. Often the longer route will also raise opportunities to clear the fear that surrounds our pathway to our soul purpose.

This is another way of seeing how Divine Will is in alignment with our need to find our soul or core purpose. Being aware that we are Source, living in a three dimensional experience, allows us to face our challenges from an appreciative state bringing us greater harmony on our soul or core mission. We achieve our soul purpose while experiencing peace and happiness.

Active Awareness Action

The greatest step we can take to help us recognise our soul purpose is to be present. If we are present we are automatically in line with our soul or core purpose. *Call in Mary Magdalena and/or Tara to help you to stay grounded and in the present.*

Surround yourself with the energy of the sacred shape; the octahedron surrounded by the sphere. Acknowledge that the vibration of the number nine is around you. This vibration is always drawn to you when you are in alignment with your soul purpose. Sit quietly in this space and allow your challenges and resulting emotions to be explored in an objective way. An example would be; if your fear of public speaking is hindering your driving need to share your enlightened wisdom with others, imagine how you would feel if you were someone who loved talking to a crowd. Allow yourself to feel the joy they feel, the excitement, the sheer love of it. Finally see yourself speaking with those same emotions of joy, confidence and excitement. The feeling of joy is your birth right from Source:

Source does not recognise fear.

Power Animal

The white husky and the hare resonate with the number nine.

Call in the energy of the white husky or the hare, whichever you are drawn to. Imagine being one with these power animals, running and exploring the unknown, filled with joy and excitement, appreciating everything in their pathway. Allow these power animals to help you feel anticipation for the future, free from fear. Do this as often as is needed until you find that you look at the next challenge without fear and instead view it with excitement and determination to go forward towards your soul purpose. As all reality is now and now is your soul purpose, understand that each step, each moment is your soul purpose.

Your soul purpose exists in every moment.

SOUL JOURNEY GUIDANCE
NINE

source energy pattern
ONE + EIGHT

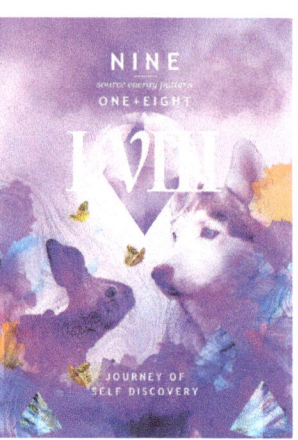

Journey of Self Discovery

We draw the strong source vibrational pattern of the number nine towards us when we are asking the question:

'Who am I?' 'I am' is the answer.

A further question can be: "what does that mean?"

The understanding of this could be aligned with being on a quest. This is the journey of self discovery.

We could ask a little child the question "who are you?" and they would reply with perhaps their name or even their gender "I am a little girl". We could ask a grown man or woman and they will also probably reply with their name and even add in their county or home town.

If we asked a distinguished person he/she may reply with their official title: an example "I am Ruth Wilson, the sister on this ward". In all walks of life, we are given titles; Mr, Mrs or Ms, Captain, Lord and Lady, Bishop, Doctor, Professor and many more. When we are asked "who are you?" we will always be able to identify ourselves.

This is because we have personality labels; first to make it easy to identify us and then more labels to identify our qualities and finally our achievements, especially if they are recognised by many. A favourite label is our age, often to be seen after the name when exposed in the media.

If we identify strongly with our material body and that which we have or have not achieved, it will affect how we see ourselves and others. This is not who we are in our wholeness. This is our ego personality self, it is our three dimensional self that manages this temporary body.

We need to first understand what we are not in order to start our lifelong journey of who we are. There are many layers and perspectives on our journey of self discovery.

The first one is to realise that any of the titles or achievements are as temporary as our material body. In fact they may only be significant for a phase of our life on Earth. This could mean if we identify ourselves with an achievement or title and it is taken from us, we could feel devastated and even worthless. However, as we start realising that we are a part of something that is universal, that we are part of something that connects all life, everything in existence, we are knowingly on the journey of self discovery.

This journey will never end but rather opens doors to many opportunities to be whatever we want to be, to limitless possibilities if we choose to explore. So, the incredible truth is that in any given moment we can discover self, or source self, and that being aware of this self in the present moment is who we are.

We can choose to be whoever we want to be in each moment. We are limitless because we are Source, and that is the key to the never ending journey of self discovery

"I am source self on a journey of limitless possibilities".

It is the process of spiritual awakening that is the journey of self discovery.

Active Awareness Action

Walk through your day in a totally present state. Be aware of your body and breath and the sounds around you. Do not be hard on yourself if your thoughts wander, gently bring yourself back to the present. This is a wonderful way to keep yourself grounded and connected. These moments, minutes and finally hours of being present are your route to self discovery giving you the freedom to choose the journey you want. Mary Magdalena and Tara will help you to do this.

Further Action

Surround yourself with the sacred shape, the octahedron surrounded by a sphere. Take time to experience its vibrational energy.

Once you feel your connection with this shape start using the powerful expression of who you are. I am ..... Follow the power of who you are by positive statements. An example would be; "I am unconditional love" or "I am more than I ever thought I could be".

Allow yourself to flow into the words so the words become an expression of who you are.

From this space you will find that the endless possibilities and choices are understood from a higher perspective. This is your wise source self discovering a greater part of itself.

Power Animal

The hare resonates with the number nine.

Allow the innate wisdom of the power animal the hare to fill you, giving you the understanding of all the possibilities that are perfect for you.

Recognise self through the mantra "I am that I am."

SOUL JOURNEY GUIDANCE
NINE

source energy pattern
TWO + SEVEN

Ready to make a Life Commitment

When we draw this image it is a universal sign that we are on the pathway to making a life commitment. This may be on a conscious or unconscious level. We will be attracting the pattern of two+seven of number nine. Each of our soul journeys will bring us towards life changing commitments.

Important life commitments can occur in personal relationships, career choices, different religions and spiritual goals. It may be a personal commitment to others or towards a situation; it can be a group commitment to another group. We often hear politicians and world leaders talking about commitment to their cause and country.

These are examples of 'life commitments' and they are also a soul commitment and an important soul growth opportunity.

Life commitments often include a ceremony and vows given or exchanged (as in marriage). It is how we view a commitment that is important. Certain commitments are for a phase of time in our life, others are meant to last our linear life, even lifetimes.

It is said that some vows or life commitments can carry through many lifetimes and can affect us on many levels. This in itself shows that a life commitment has to be taken seriously, it needs to be from the heart and that could mean that it is another soul lesson in unconditional love, compassion and authenticity.

To make a life commitment, all of these qualities will be part of this choice. This is because life commitments are the essence of all that is. They are helping the understanding that we are all part of Source. Every commitment to others is also a commitment to ourselves.

Where we may find it difficult is where we are not in alignment with our source self. An example of this would be if others are guiding us towards a commitment that does not feel right for us. Our reluctance can often take us by surprise, as it could be that we have suppressed our true feelings and now have to face them.

To face a life commitment is to have compassion. This holds the passion and the unconditional attention of love that is needed for the intended commitment.

Next, we need to give the authenticity of our true selves to the commitment. This means that we need to feel free from the fear of commitment and act as if we are baring our souls to scrutiny. Our thoughts, feelings and actions need to be at peace and we need to feel at one with the commitment.

We can only be so if the decision is a higher heart knowing, free from the pressure of outside influences; these influences can be cultural, religious, spiritual or even a fear of displeasing those we care for. They can stem from a fear of loss - a loss of love, social standing or being alone.

Being ready for a life commitment is being free from fear towards the life commitment. However, the lessons and understanding of our authentic self in getting ready to make the decision is what draws the loving vibrational energy of the number nine towards us in the vibrational pattern of two+seven. The vibration of this particular pattern will help us to feel the guidance of Source. It helps us to understand any misgivings at a core level.

Active Awareness Action

Meditating will always help you to be objective about an impending life commitment.

Find a quiet place, connect with Mary Magdalena and/or Tara and draw in the energy and strength of the sacred shape the octahedron, with a surrounding sphere.

This sacred shape will help you to stay firmly grounded and connected to the present, to the life within and without. This shape will keep you in alignment with the vibration of the number nine and its pattern two+seven.

You may be drawn to hold a piece of labradorite. The energy of this crystal will help to clear the confusion and chaos in your thoughts. This will help you to declutter your mind and allow you to see your future commitment free from anxiety. You will see the potential to your spiritual wellbeing more clearly.

Power Animal

The white husky resonates with the number nine.

The tenacity and presence of the white husky will help you to discover aspects of your authenticity that you have perhaps hidden from yourself. Breathe in the wisdom of this power animal and allow it to help you to see the intended life commitment from your own wise self, your source self.

Life commitments are soul choices.

SOUL JOURNEY GUIDANCE
NINE

source energy pattern
THREE + SIX

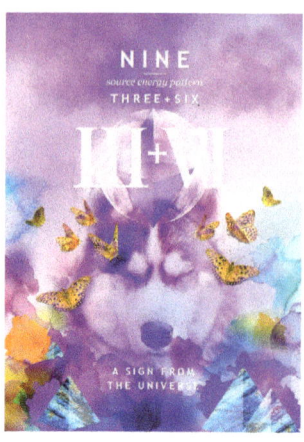

A Sign from the Universe

The universe speaks to us in many different ways. It communicates with us in ways that are perfectly right at any one moment. We need to be able to interpret what is communicated to us. We need to understand the deeper meaning and allow it to expand as our awareness grows.

What is a sign from the universe?

A sign from the universe is a response from Source. It is one of the clearest signals that we, as human beings, can receive to remind us that we have in fact manifested a higher guidance that is from Source. *Take a moment to contemplate that you are a source being within a human material body. That being the case you, at a soul level, are also responsible for that source filled sign. This does not make it any less wondrous to see or experience. In fact, it is empowering to realise that you are part of creating universal signs.*

If, however it feels better to ask the angelic beings or Source itself from a subjective place to bring forward a sign to help us, that is also perfectly right. Some universal signs can be life changing or just a gentle prodding in certain areas of our life. Many times, universal signs are synchronistic happenings that make us aware that there is something greater than our personality selves.

Synchronicity is a word coined by Carl Jung, a Swiss psychiatrist, implying a 'meaningful coincidence'.

These 'meaningful coincidences' seem to happen frequently when we start awakening to our source selves; however, this is because as it happens more regularly we accept it as a normal coincidence of source alignment.

When we find the right wisdom course or speak to a wise person who will help us on the next stage of our spiritual journey in the most unexpected places, we are appreciative but not surprised.

The truth is that Source is communicating and guiding us constantly in the way of synchronistic happenings, various signs and even miracles. We can see miracles as the purest universal sign of manifesting in perfect alignment with Source. These pure universal signs change personal lives and can have an effect on countless people.

Signs from the universe are limitless, as are the possibilities of Source. Though there are some well known indications that the universe is communicating with us, such as white feathers or we see a sequence of numbers in unusual places, for instance, eleven minutes past the eleventh hour on a clock face.

However, there are times when our thoughts and emotions cloud our judgement and we are confused and fearful of our choices or decisions.

We may then ask for clear signs that will help us. It is often at these times that we are surrounded in the pattern three+six of the number nine and the sign will be a powerful happening that may jolt us in an uncomfortable way. This is because the gentle sign was not enough to help us see another direction, choice or decision.

These unsettling signs are huge gifts from Source but may not always be appreciated at the time. An example can be of an elderly couple who love their family country home and are reluctant to leave. They keep praying and asking for guidance.

Then there is an unusually thick unexpected snowfall and they are completely cut off. The local farmer comes to their rescue with his tractor. They had received their answer. They moved close to town and the shops. It can be said that it was a gift from the universe in that they were finally clear about what their next step should be.

If we accept that we and the Universe are one we can expect to experience the Divine within and without to communicate with us.

Active Awareness Action

When you need a sign from the Universe (from Source) make sure that you are filled with the gratitude of one who has already received and allow yourself to be open to any sign or synchronistic happening. Mary Magdalena and Tara will help you here. A short daily meditation during which you express your gratitude for what you have and for what you desire will increase your openness to receive. Keep your thoughts of gratitude focused and clear but always with the intention that you are open to receive what is perfect for your highest good.

Power Animal

The white husky resonates with the number nine.

This power animal will help you to be constantly in the present moment so that you are open to receiving signs from the universe.

Source gives us signs for our soul journey.

SOUL JOURNEY GUIDANCE
NINE

source energy pattern
FOUR + FIVE

Spiritual Discipline

Spiritual growth is achieved when we take
responsibility for our life and happiness
Taking responsibility for your happiness and for the
happenings in your life will attract the pattern four+five
of the number nine towards you in a conscious manner.
From a young age we are taught the first steps towards taking responsibility. Little tasks
that, as we grow older, become more towards training us to be independent and take on
the responsibility for looking after ourselves.

Taking responsibility for ourselves is also about being responsible for our own happiness,
for making choices and decisions that bring us fulfilment and joy. This is wonderful all the
time that life is good for us; however, when chaos and disruption fill our life it is very easy to
blame others including our partners, work colleagues, anyone who we feel has contributed
to our unhappy experience. We may also blame the circumstances, even political leaders.

This thought process leads to a victim mindset and although this can elicit compassion
from others, which is soothing and even healing, it takes away our own personal power.
We become puppets to life, we hand over the reins of life to others.

This is a journey guidance which will resonate with many of us at some time on
our life journey. This pattern will help us to recognise this and it is our own free will that
allows us to choose empowerment by taking responsibility for ourselves.

When we take responsibility for our lives we are not only empowered but we can
create our reality to be whatever we wish to be. This is true empowerment. This means
that we can choose to be happy, content, abundant, healthy and live a fulfilling life.

To do this we need to look at our thought processes. This is the huge step towards
empowering ourselves. Once we take responsibility for our thoughts we are able to
examine them from a detached place. This allows us to change our thoughts to thought
patterns that enhance our lives. When we have taken control of our lives and no longer
live life as a victim we are ready to look at our spiritual lives.

Our spiritual growth depends on our spiritual discipline. In order to walk each day
in the present moment, being fully connected to our source selves, takes discipline and
love for ourselves.

To be spiritually disciplined is to be in alignment with the will of Source.
To love ourselves is to be able to forgive ourselves if we fail in our endeavour to be
constantly conscious.

One well used excuse is "I do not have time to consciously connect to Source". That same excuse is often used for other spiritual practices, an example would be a daily meditation. This is once more laying blame and not taking responsibility for our own time management.

Ask yourself these questions:

Do I love myself enough to make time to invest in my spiritual practices?

Am I avoiding the commitment that this needs?

How important is my spiritual growth to me?

Take time with each question and then listen from your heart to your response.

Active Awareness Action

Decide that you are going to self empower yourself. Write down the parts of your life where you feel that others are to blame or you feel disempowered. This is an important step to clarify your feelings. Call on Mary Magdalena and Tara to help you.

To guide and help you call on the energy of the sacred source filled octahedron surrounded by a sphere to enable you to see clearly where you can step into your power.

You can also use labradorite or moonstone to help you to attune to Mother Earth and your own physical form, which in turn, connects you to your higher self (source self) and Source. Be aware of staying in the present and consider once more what you can do to remove the blame from others, situations and circumstances. Sense how strong you feel.

It is only when you stop blaming life and what it brings you that you can make changes.

Power Animal

The white husky resonates with the number nine.

If you are drawn to the energy of the white husky, breathe in its powerful energy. From this place feel free from guilt and blame.

Spend time in this powerful energy and feel how in tune with Source you feel. You are ready to take responsibility for your thoughts, your actions and any situation you find yourself in.

Once you take responsibility you are an apprentice master taking control of your destiny.

Responsibility leads to spiritual growth.

SOUL JOURNEY GUIDANCE
ELEVEN

You are the Law of Attraction

Power animal: Snow Leopard

Sacred shape: Twelve Pointed Star
surrounded by a Sphere

Master: Maitreya

Crystal: Amethyst

The power animal resonating with the vibration of the number eleven is the snow leopard.

The shape that will help us to connect to the vibrational energy of the number eleven is a twelve pointed star (stellated dodecahedron) surrounded by a sphere.

The crystal that carries the vibration of Maitreya and of the number eleven is the amethyst.

Soul Journey Number Eleven

The **law of attraction** is the fundamental process of the quantum vibration of this planet Earth. It is also known as the **law of mirroring**. This description is closer to the truth of how this law of Source works. When we draw this image or feel a pull towards the vibration of the number eleven we will find that we are being asked to look at what we are mirroring or attracting into our spiritually evolving life that is not in alignment with our source self needs/desires.

We create our reality on the outside from the projections of our inner selves. The projections are our thoughts and emotional expressions. These can be from our subconscious or body memory which means our projections are completely subjective and so our thoughts and actions are not always in line with our source selves.

Consequently, through the law of attraction we draw in or attract from the universe that which we are projecting. This means we are often creating our future from a distorted place of confusion and chaos. However, this is an immense soul growth journey; we are creators (as we are Source) and we can create Heaven or extreme challenges for ourselves. We are helped on many levels and if we are prompted by our source self to look at what we are mirroring in our lives we will be surrounded by the strong vibration of the number eleven to be more aware of our thought patterns. We have all heard people say: "Why am I having such a hard time?" or "Why do I keep attracting the same type of person to me?" "Life is unfair." or "Why is this happening to me?" We will identify with these responses either from a detached awareness or from victim mode (when we feel that we have no say in our future.)

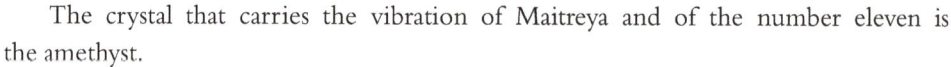

This is the time to ask ourselves: '*Do I regularly have the same painful or unsettled thoughts and feelings?*' If so we need to look at the cause of our emotional dis-ease. This takes integrity and commitment to want to change that which we are drawing towards us. .

The first step

We need to want to change our predictable future because we are weary of drawing in the same experience.

Second step

We need to spend time in quiet awareness, which encourages the understanding of why we keep having the same negative thoughts and feelings. When we have found the cause of these feelings, we need to acknowledge and detach from them.

Active Awareness Action

In a quiet secluded place, allow yourself time to be still, relaxed and present. Write down your habitual thoughts that affect you in an adverse way. Breathe in the energy of Maitreya and allow his wisdom to fill you. You will find random thoughts and feelings will arrive, write them down or record them. Once you have understood why you have these patterns and subsequent emotions. Ask yourself: Am I understanding and gaining insights from my source self or my fearful ego personality? This is an important question as the more honest you are with yourself the more easily you will see the bigger picture of why you have these fearful thoughts. Honesty can be subjective and in order to get to a more objective, honest, insight untainted by the ego personality's fear, you need time to raise your energetic vibration and be firmly present in order to trust your insights.

Now ask yourself: what am I learning from this? followed by: do I want to attract a better future for myself? Write down what you want in the future and the steps you need to take to achieve this. How would you feel if you achieved this? This is the key to attracting what you want; you need to feel the resultant emotion as if you already have the desired outcome. Place yourself within the source filled energy of a twelve pointed star surrounded with a sphere. This will give you a strong connection to the vibration of number eleven, which will help you to sustain the feeling of joyful success that you desire in your future.

Power Animal

The snow leopard resonates with the number eleven.

This power animal will help you to own the reality of what you create, in other words for you to see that you are attracting a vibrational match to yourself whether it be another person, a situation or the future. Call in and surround yourself with the energy of the snow leopard. Acknowledge the resilience of this power animal and the compassion it feels for your life journey. You will be free from judgement and will instead move forward with positive thoughts for your future.

Positive thoughts attract a positive future.

SOUL JOURNEY GUIDANCE
ELEVEN

source energy pattern
TWO + NINE

The Art of Manifestation

To manifest is the process we use whilst understanding the vibrational energy of the law of attraction.

To Manifest is to Create

When we intend to manifest we attract the pattern two+nine of the number eleven. This source energy pattern helps us to understand that we are part of the creator and thus able to create. In order to manifest we need to be clear about what we want. This is very important as most of us dwell on what we do not want or do not have, which draws us towards those unwanted realities. This is reflected in that well known saying 'what you resist persists' (Carl Jung). It is a universal truth.

We need to remember that the Universe does not recognise the negative article. If your thought says 'do not want' the Universe will respond to that thought by giving you what you do not want.

Next, we need to understand that the surrounding reality is what we have attracted. We need to accept this and not lay the blame on others or past deeds. We are creators and we manifest through powerful positive intention. This needs to be clear so we may need some time to decide what we want to manifest.

We need to make what we desire so real that we can see it clearly in our minds. We must capture that feeling, or emotion. It may be joy, contentment, excitement or perhaps peace. We then allow the feeling to fill us. We are creating a vibrational match to what we want and desire which in turn draws it towards us. Any negative thoughts that oppose this vibrational match, will adversely affect our manifestation.

We do not need to concern ourselves with how we receive our intended manifestation, only trust that we will receive. We can manifest anything we want. This includes such things as the perfect career, the home that we love, the soulmate, a positive situation, even a car or a holiday. Restrictions persist if we do not think we deserve it or we do not trust the universe of which we are all part.

Active Awareness Action

Start with your intention. What is it you desire? Be clear about what you want, it helps to write down what you want in detail. Use your imagination, which is a powerful creating tool. See what you desire in your mind. Make it as detailed as possible, a visualisation of what you want.

You need to feel as if you already have what you desire. Allow all your senses to help you with this. (Maybe your desired want has a smell or special texture or even a sound).

Do this visualisation combined with how you feel every day for about 5-10 minutes. It must not be a chore but a delight. It is exciting to create. Remember that you can be open to the universe giving you more than you desire as there are endless possibilities that you may not have considered.

Express gratitude for receiving what you already have as you visualise your desire. Act in a way that your desire will be with you any day.

An example is if you wanted to move home, start sorting your things and decluttering to get ready for the move. An example of manifesting may be the home of your dreams.

First you would be clear about what you wanted, in detail. You can draw it so it is easier to imagine (visualisation). With your intention feel what it would be like to be living there (creating in the present moment). This is the key to manifesting.

Feel grateful for what you have already received in your life as you spend five minutes every day visualising your new home, feeling and experiencing the emotions that you feel when you have your new home.

Now is the time to do things that are conducive to moving (acting with intention) for example you may cost prices for removal men. This is drawing towards you the home which is a vibrational match.

This is how you use the law of attraction to manifest your desire.

Maitreya will help you with your focus and the integrity of your desire. Place yourself in the sacred shape of the twelve pointed star surrounded by a sphere, which will help with your focus and the integrity of your desire.

Power Animal

The snow leopard resonates with the number eleven.

If you feel drawn to the snow leopard surround yourself with its energy. This will help you to feel the gratitude for what you already have. It is this gratitude that places you in the space of receiving, which in turn draws towards you that which you desire.

Creation is the result of manifestation.

SOUL JOURNEY GUIDANCE
ELEVEN

source energy pattern
THREE + EIGHT

Be an Observer

Life can be seen as a 'merry go round' and we often refer to the 'carousel of life'. Imagine that our personality self is the carousel. The selection of different seats on this carousel is our thinking mind's processes which are an extension of our personality/ego self.

We can change to a different thought, that is a different seat on the carousel; however, if we are unaware that the mind and ego self are controlling us we simply stay on the carousel of our personality self until our growing spiritual awareness enables us to realise we can choose to get off the carousel. If we get off, we become aware that there is more to us than our endless thoughts.

We become an observer, watching and hearing the personality self, but from a place where we can detach. We are aware that we are not only the thinking mind but that we can also detach and observe. This analogy shows that we are personality or ego self and yet so much more. We are Source.

Once we understand that we are Source we can then begin to control our thoughts and thought patterns and not let the mind control us. We can step off the carousel and be an observer of our mental and emotional responses to our external reality. This empowers us to understand that to follow our fearful thoughts and indulge in being a victim leaves us powerless. Instead we can choose to detach by understanding the thought processes that are not in alignment with our source self. This is part of our soul growth.

It is this pattern three+eight of the number eleven that is attracted to us when we are committed to being an observer. We need to accept that from our ego self, all our thoughts are subjective in terms of perceiving our reality. The true reality is in the moment. Everything else is a memory or a future desire. We must allow the observer in us to use the memories that are filled with wisdom and the gratitude in our hearts to create our perfect future reality; to face any soul lessons we have put in place.

A simple way to be an observer is to meditate. This is because through mindful meditation we are in the present moment consciously. The art to being an observer is not to be judgmental towards any thoughts. These are projections of the personality self which will flood our thoughts.

When a thought, or a pattern of thoughts come in, acknowledge the thought. Is it a thought that is positive and fulfilling? Or does it come from a place of anxiety or concern? Bear in mind all negative thoughts have a core of fear and that negative thoughts are also subjective in terms of perceiving our own reality.

An example could be: If two people, in the same external circumstances, needed to move home, they could each experience this from a totally different point of view.

One person may see the move as full of anxious challenges and thereby project a sense of fearfulness. The other may see the move as exciting, a new venture and would project a totally different reality.

Let us become an observer and change our reality to one of peace and acceptance, which is the basis for happiness and contentment.

Active Awareness Action

Find a peaceful place, in nature or somewhere where you will not be disturbed. You may want to surround yourself with the twelve pointed star surrounded by a sphere giving you a strong connection to the vibration of the number eleven.

Focus on your breath. Breathe in time with your body's rhythm. This means it should feel perfectly right for you. Be completely mindful of your surroundings, the sounds and smells, then take your attention to your body, whilst using your breath to breathe in light and breathe out all limitations. The growing awareness of your light filled body is what grounds and connects you to Source.

Become an observer and from this space allow the thoughts to come in, acknowledge and then let them go. You can help further by, in your mind, making statements like, 'that is an angry thought' or 'that is a loving thought'.

Source is observing, noticing, free from judgement. Start with 10 minutes a day until you are ready to do longer. You will find that you are taking control of your thoughts and mind. This in itself brings peace.

Power Animal

The snow leopard resonates with the number eleven.

In your meditation become the snow leopard. Prowl and leap from rock to rock. You will be present and yet filled with the fortitude and the willpower to make the commitments; to acknowledge that you are Source and in control of your mind and body. This power animal can take you on a journey that presents different ways to achieve this. Be open to the energy of the snow leopard.

Observe from the perspective of your source self.

SOUL JOURNEY GUIDANCE
ELEVEN

source energy pattern
FOUR + SEVEN

Raising our Vibration Protects us

Raising the frequency of our vibrational energy protects us.

When we attract this image, it may mean that we need to consider changes in our physical and spiritual lifestyle. What are we doing to raise the frequency of our vibrational energy? Do we have a daily focus on raising our frequency and thereby increasing our vibrational energy?

This is extremely important as our vibrational frequency is in direct response to how we are feeling at any given moment. When we feel happy, contented and peaceful this will reflect in our energetic aura. However, if we feel unhappy or fearful this too will affect our energetic aura. Our feelings are a result of our thoughts. This will include all feelings of light from joy, ecstasy and contentment to those that are dark with fear, anger and resentment.

Ways to raise our frequency and so Increase our vibrational energy:

Positive thoughts: most importantly we need to monitor our thoughts. We must become aware of our thoughts and thought patterns through our responsive feelings.

How much of your day do you spend feeling at peace with yourself? This is a vital question to our future wellbeing. We need to fill our days with positive, uplifting, creative thoughts that become our reality.

Meditate: consider a daily undisturbed meditation from fifteen minutes, to as long as is needed. This helps us to observe our thoughts in a detached, non-judgemental manner, which in turn helps us to master our thoughts so they are in alignment with Source.

Nature: spend time in nature. Nature is an example of Source in its purest interpretation. We will find that walking in forests where we can hear the sounds of birds and the wind in the trees will automatically increase our energetic frequency.

Music: listen to calming music. Any music that fills us with joy will raise our vibrational energy.

Source filled breath: focused breathing methods, which we enjoy, will raise our frequency.

Water: think how much pleasure we feel when we soak in a bath or have a refreshing shower. Equally, on an energetic level, the water will cleanse us and raise our vibration.

Nurture: acts of love and compassion to others and to ourselves will increase our vibrational frequency.

Laughter: laughter is a release of joyously qualified energy that not only raises our vibrational frequency but will affect those around us as well.

Energy food: eat high vibrational foods that we enjoy. Blessing our food raises the vibrational frequency of our food.

Exercise: exercise will release chemicals called endorphins which trigger a feeling of euphoria. They are often called the body's 'natural happy drug'. Most importantly we need to choose a form of exercise we enjoy. This may be walking, yoga, dancing, exercise classes or marathons.

Spiritual guidance: reading spiritually informative books or listening to inspiring and wise teachers will affect our frequency, as will positive affirmations.

Gratitude: feeling blessed and grateful for our physical bodies and our life on Mother Earth will always raise our energetic vibration.

These are a few of the favourite methods of raising the frequency of our vibrational energy.

The inclusive key to all of these suggestions is being fully present and mindful while feeling alive with the joy of the activity.

Our intention to raise our energetic vibration is what draws the pattern four+seven of the number eleven towards us, especially when we are walking in nature, experiencing water, or using our breath in a focused manner, with a passion for life.

Raising the frequency of our vibrational energy can protect us spiritually.

When we are masters of our intentions and no longer in victim mode, we will realise that one of the strongest ways to protect ourselves spiritually from external negativity is to raise our vibrational energy.

Like attracts like.

If we are constantly aware of our thoughts and keep ourselves spiritually cleansed and vibrating at a high frequency we will attract similar.

Our own high vibrational state is the best spiritual protection we can have.

Keep in mind that there is no problem with using different methods to protect ourselves, an example may be calling in a sphere of source light.

However, we need to be aware of our motivation for calling in a particular tool of spiritual protection.

Is it from fear and being a victim? Or from the knowing that we are apprentice Masters?

Our Mantra is:

I am Light
I am Love
I am a Being of Light and Love
I am Light
I am Love
I am a Sphere of Light and Love

When we keep our vibrational energy high we are protected purely because we only attract what is equal to us.

Have you noticed the positive affect you have on others when you are feeling wonderful and content?

This is because as we increase our vibrational frequency we can affect others energy in the same way that other high vibrational people, happenings or nature have affected us.

Active Awareness Action

The master Maitreya will help you to draw in the pattern four+seven. Surround yourself with a twelve pointed star surrounded by a sphere. Using your breath, breathe in the source vibration of eleven, feel the Source within you tingle, feel how pure and light you feel. Stay in this space for as long as you need.

Power Animal

The snow leopard resonates with the number eleven.

Allow the snow leopard to show you how to be present in every moment, fully conscious of everything you do.

Feel Life. Feel Alive.

SOUL JOURNEY GUIDANCE
ELEVEN

source energy pattern
FIVE + SIX

Appreciation leads to Happiness

One of the most significant ways of expressing our source self is through appreciation. When gratitude is felt for something or someone and we feel it in the presence of our source self, this is the act of appreciation; a fully present awareness of what we are grateful for. When we express gratitude, we are in the light of grace.

The words 'thank you' carry a high vibration and will positively affect whoever we are thanking. Most of us, at some time or other in our day, say those words. We can say it casually, or with a deep felt feeling of gratitude which resonates through us and is shown in our energy field as a higher frequency.

When we say 'thank you', whether it be for a small act of consideration or for a larger act of kindness or compassion, it will be meaningless unless we are fully present in our expression of gratitude.

Gratitude is something we often express when we have moved forward from a challenging or disappointing time. This will often mean that when we are expressing our gratitude it will still hold the memory and energy flow of the low emotions we have experienced.

However, if we look at the situation as a lesson and find the blessing within the challenge, the gratitude we feel for that blessing is what changes the frequency of that emotion. When we are experiencing the grace of appreciation we are in our source selves. We are responding from our source self.

To appreciate is to be fully present and it comes from a place of feeling blessed. To feel happy can only be achieved by being fully present. We can think about happy events in the past and remember how that felt and we can imagine how it would feel to be happy in the future. However, neither are the reality of the present moment unless we are fully present in that feeling of happiness.

It is the emotion of gratitude in the awareness of our appreciation that leads us to happiness. It is this act of appreciation that draws in the vibration of the pattern five+six of the number eleven.

There are tools and ways to make us feel happy; however, if we go to the core of everything that creates that feeling of joy, wellbeing, gratitude and in turn happiness we will find appreciation. In other words, happiness is appreciation and appreciation is happiness, the difference is merely in the perception.

A child feels happiness not always aware of appreciating the happening, an adult is aware of appreciating but may not always see the happiness in the happening.

Take time to consider this and experiment with this concept.

Appreciation can express itself in emotions of joy, compassion, excitement, optimism, wonder, even anticipation. The greatest emotional aspect of appreciation is love. We cannot be present, filled with the emotion of love and not feel happy.

Active Awareness Action

If we choose this image we need to ask ourselves these questions:

What do I appreciate in my life?

Are there people in my life that make me feel appreciative?

Do I look for blessings hidden in my life challenges?

Do I wake up feeling happy?

Does my happiness depend on others?

If a question feels too simple or you feel the need to dismiss it, it may mean you need to take the time to question the motive behind this.

Think further on this question: Do I wake up feeling happy? The fact is that those few minutes that you take to wake up can affect your whole days wellbeing.

Be mindful of how important those first few minutes are to set your day's journey into one of happiness and peace.

Spend those waking moments infusing yourself with the vibration of everything you appreciate about yourself and your life.

Power Animal

The snow leopard resonates with the number eleven.

Work with the snow leopard in the twelve pointed star surrounded by a sphere. Take the questions from above and spend time on each question. All the time, this shape is helping you to express gratitude. The snow leopard is helping you to see the lessons in your life and allowing you to appreciate what you have learnt.

Happiness is found in the present moment.

Method Four: Soul Journey Birth Day Numbers

The birth day number is also important. This is the number for the appropriate day of the month when a person was born.

For instance, the person born on 29.12.1999 has a number of 29 as they were born on the 29 day of December. Whereas the child born on 5 May 2018 has a number of 5 as they were born on the 5 day of May and their sibling born on 4.9.2016 has a number of 4 as they were born on the 4 day of September. The mother of the children has a number of 30 as she was born on the 30 day of June.

To calculate the soul journey birth day number the two numbers are added together, so our person born on 29.12.1999 has 29 as they were born on the 29 day of the month of December, and when we add the 2 and 9 together, we get 11, which is their birthday number.

The pensioner born on 21 June 1940 has the number 21 giving 3 as their birth day number when we add the two numbers together.

The mother was born on 30 June 1988, giving her number as 3 + 0 = 3 and their father, born on 2 February 1983 has a birth day number of 2.

If you were born on 11 or 29 your birth day number will be 11.

When you have completed this for your own date of birth and calculated your own birth day number:

1. Read the relevant section on your birth energy (pages 85 to 94).

2. Look for the appropriate image.
The image will show the power animal, the shape and the crystal for that particular number.

When you have absorbed the energy of the appropriate image, look at the number within this book to gain further insights into the particular power animal, its qualities and how it is helping and supporting you.

Your birth day number gives you the power animal that was present on the day that you were born, this very special day when you incarnated on planet Earth and took your first breath, your first experience of life on Earth outside the womb.

We incarnate on planet Earth to experience life here, to clear any karmic debt that we have brought forward from past lives, to clear any energy blocks that we have with us, and to learn and grow on our own unique soul journey. Your birth day power animal will help and support you with all of this, so really get to know them, spend time appreciating every aspect of their being and acknowledge all the help and support they are giving to you.

If your Birth Day Energy is the Number One

ONE

COMPLETION BRINGING
NEW BEGINNINGS

When you have the number one as your birth day energy vibration, you can expect your life to have many wonderful opportunities for soul growth. These constant and often uplifting changes and challenges help you to remember you are a Being of Source, someone who can create their own reality.

When you are in alignment with Source your courage knows no bounds, you can take on the world, your enthusiasm for any new idea is infectious, you will take control in a balanced understanding way.

You will often come forward with radical new ways and methods that can have a huge effect on your working or home life.

Your strongest healing is done with people who have lost their way, your understanding and empathy often changes peoples' lives.

You can get bored, but this is generally your soul promoting you onwards. If you are not in alignment with your source self, boredom can lead you to do things that perhaps have unhappy consequences and in these situations you need to move forward or change direction otherwise your inhibiting fear can cause chaos.

However, you are strong and generally an honest and honourable soul and if you have caused distress to others this will often make you stop and make radical changes to undo the hurt and pain. Huge lessons and soul growth can come from these uncomfortable times.

Taking committed steps to realign yourself with your higher intuition and source self enables you to travel through these times with far greater ease and grace. You can shake yourself like a wet dog, getting rid of hurts and pain without hanging on to the past.

When in alignment with Source your ability to move forward after huge challenges, with clear vision and determination, can be a great comfort to those who share their life with you.

You have a wonderful sense of humour and can laugh at the idiosyncrasies in life without becoming bitter.

You love life!!

If your Birth Day Energy is the Number Two

Having the birth day vibration of the number two will generally mean that your life journey is about many types of relationships.

Some people who carry this vibration, start from a young age dealing with either sibling challenges or even find themselves in dysfunctional families. Foster parents or adoption can be part of their lives and often huge soul growth is made at an early age. This can be a blessing in disguise.

Adoption and fostering would come easily to you as an adult if this is your soul plan.

You will have done this journey before in many lives and in this life you may need to clear the karma to help you to move forward. This is often the case if you are attracted to the same type of person, whether it a partner or friend, that causes you dis-ease.

This is a result of being out of alignment with your source self. When you are out of alignment, your heart may be broken many times, you are deeply sensitive to others unkindness and will take each slight personally which can lead to painful unhappiness.

Often this is when the universe sends the perfect person as a friend, this may even be a next door neighbour, who has a message for you, or they may introduce you to a workshop or talk that becomes a key to your own deep wisdom.

As an old soul in this soul lifetime you will find it easy to help others. You will be the one that, even as a teenager, is able to see other people's relationship challenges with understanding and wisdom. You are the perfect agony aunt even at a young age. When you are aware of your source self and are constantly grounded and connected, you will understand why others can be so unseeing in their relationships, and will have an overwhelming need to help them.

You are perfectly balanced in a one to one counselling or wisdom guidance session and if this is part of your soul path, you will excel at it. In the workplace and within your home life, you will be the intermediary who calms situations between family members, work mates or even bigger work disputes. You can always bring harmony to the situation.

Your soul plan may be to be a leader and this will only be challenging if you are unaware of your source self, otherwise you will be able to see all view points and be able to lead in a balanced, kind but firm manner.

Your wisdom and deep understanding of many types of personalities enables you to lead in a peaceful but inspirational manner. You love being in love and your friendships are important to you. When you are in alignment with Source you are a charismatic person that can bring huge light and understanding into every relationship.

If your Birth Day Energy is the Number Three

Having the birth day vibration of the number three means that your soul journey is one of Christ Conscious awareness and finding joy in your life. You will constantly be seeking knowledge, which will lead you to courses, higher education and studies. It is often later on in life that your own source wisdom awareness enlightens your knowledge and combined with the deep understanding of your source self, will enable you to serve others in a more profound way.

You will often be drawn to positions where you are guiding or counselling others. Your connection to your source self will be strong and will help you to work in a loving compassionate way with children who have difficulties or special needs. They may not know what they need, but your strong connection to your source self and theirs, will be invaluable in finding ways forward. Children are drawn to you, and so are animals. You have the potential to be a 'horse whisperer' or a 'dog whisperer'. If it is part of your soul journey you will help many distressed animals; you will find that you can communicate with them on a higher level.

When you are in sync with your source self you are free of judgement and you will find that you see the Christ Consciousness more easily in others. This enables you to help them to see themselves in a positive loving light.

You have the potential to be a strong energy healer and you will often be drawn to many types of energy healing. This can lead to a slight confusion and questioning. At these times remain as grounded and connected as you can and allow your source self to lead you to the correct healing modality for you. It is not that various healing modalities are wrong, it is just that your source self will resonate profoundly with the one that is correct for you and you will feel as if you are coming home. This is what is happening when you discover the healing that you have used throughout many lifetimes because you are an old soul when it comes to healing. It will feel so familiar that you will know it is the correct one for you to be using.

When you are not in alignment you may become distressed at world events as you feel helpless and sometimes angry. This can sometimes lead you to take dramatic actions and join groups or organisations that can result in a challenging journey. This of course is still your soul journey, just more challenging than it needs to be, an uphill struggle that can make you feel weary and disillusioned.

However, your strong connection to your own Christ Consciousness and the joy you still find in little things will bring you back into alignment with Source and you will see your challenges and decisions as lessons enabling you to take this wisdom and resulting empathy and compassion into your home and work life. Your ability to forgive others is source given and this helps you to move forward without dwelling on the past. It may be that your soul journey is to help others find joy in their lives. Your life is about understanding that you are in service to Source and when you awaken to this, joy fills your life and touches others.

If your Birth Day Energy is the Number Four

When your birth day energy is the number four you will find that you are drawn to nature and Mother Earth. You will love being surrounded by the beauty of nature. Beauty will make your heart sing and you will find a deep peace and healing by being outside in the countryside.

Your spirituality is strongly connected to the Mother Divine and Divine Love. You may be drawn to gardening and if it is part of your soul journey you will find that growing plants as homeopathic remedies will be a fulfilling pastime.

You will also find that you are in tune with Mother Earth and can harmonise the energies with spiritual understanding and knowing.

Your creativity is boundless and will often reveal itself within organisational skills.

You may find your soul journey brings you into service with elderly people and you are full of respect for their wisdom and life experiences. You see past their ageing process and see them as ageless and wise.

If your soul journey blueprint is to be a spiritual leader you will be firm but kind. Your classes will be full of laughter and joy as you have an innate way of balancing the practical and the spiritual that helps people enjoy learning with you.

When you are in harmony with your source self you will find that you are never lonely. You enjoy other people's company but you are also happy in your own complete wholeness.

However, when there is disharmony this can completely change your personality and you may find yourself withdrawing from other people. You find that their noise and bluster irritates and causes you discomfort, so that you seek time by yourself.

Even partnerships can suffer from this need to be alone. This can lead to huge soul growth as you find the courage and determination to venture forth on your own. Partners may find this difficult to handle. These adventures, or even pilgrimages, give you time to become more aware of your source self and a deep connection takes place. This in turn helps you to help others who feel trapped by life.

You have innate leadership qualities and an ability, when you are in Source Conscious awareness, to know your own self worth. This allows you to bring out the best in those who you lead, as you see their self worth through source filled eyes and can gently, in a structured way, help them to move forward with confidence that is gained from seeing themselves through your eyes.

Your friendship is valued by many and your earthly, practical, but source filled wisdom is often called upon.

If your Birth Day Energy is the Number Five

Your life will be about flow and balance in the material world and also, as you become more aware, in the balance of your spiritual life.

You may feel, at times, that nowhere is home. These are times to remember to ground and connect so that you feel your source self.

You can be very influenced and connected to all that is otherworldly. You will be drawn to other, unseen mainly, different dimensional beings, such as unicorns, fairy folk etc. You will find that stories of extra terrestrial beings will interest you. Your interest will be strong whether you believe or not. The galaxy and its mysteries will fascinate you and may even draw you in to study further.

There will often be a discord or disharmony with your mystical side as you will also be extremely logical and want to learn the truth of the mysteries that surround us all.

You will find that in certain circumstances you act as a bridge between science and spiritual theories. Often scientists and spiritual gurus reach the same goal through different routes. Although it is good to be interested in both routes you may find at times you feel confused, lost and unsure. This can affect your decisions in work, studying and even relationships. People may accuse you of sitting on the fence and not having a definite opinion. However, in actual fact this is because you have a foot in each camp and can often see the truth in both.

A huge soul journey challenge is to stay as grounded and in the present as you can through meditation, nature walks and many other practices such as yoga and specific breath work. This enables you to be open minded through being constantly aware of the Source within and so able to trust where you feel there is truth.

Teaching can be something you love doing; however if you are not in harmony with your source self, you will feel trapped and often unhappy. Restlessness and feelings of not belonging can be felt when the source connection is not being felt. This is often when the soul has not had many personality lives on Earth and still has strong karma connection to other planets or universes. Being constantly grounded and connected is essential for the connection to Source and source self.

Being close to water and nature is a huge part of life and spiritual retreats in nature and self sufficiency lifestyles will often be run by those surrounded by the vibration of the number five.

When you are in harmony, you will be able to serve others in many different ways as the creative side in you is so versatile and flowing.

If your Birth Day Energy is the Number Six

If your birth day energy is the number six you will find that spiritual service to others is a huge part of your soul journey.

This does not mean that this will always be in the conventionally recognised ways. Whether you are a lawyer, medical doctor, or in any other service position, your strong connection to your own and others Source Consciousness will always influence your dealings. You will go that extra mile to help because you will know and feel that it is the right thing to do.

Your perception of people will often be without judgement. This makes it easier for you to work in service to people who have lost their way and are working against the laws of Source.

This does, however, mean that you have to be in a strong alignment with your source self otherwise you could be easily disappointed in people and hurt by their reactions.

It may be that your soul journey brings these happenings into your family life. This is in fact harder to deal with, as it is so personal. If this is the case, it makes it very important to maintain your regular spiritual practices and make time to recharge your spiritual batteries.

You will be drawn to study and may hide behind that as a reason not to step forward (the person who is always the student). When you are in full alignment with your source self you will find that you are gently guided to move forward and spread your knowledge and wisdom. This, in turn, helps you to motivate others and bring out the best in them. If it is in your soul journey to nurse others you will feel the compassion of someone that understands past ailments and disease and connects heart to heart with your patients.

You will also be drawn to working with young children and the natural joy they find in early childhood. You will be the perfect guide to allow the child/children to grow in wisdom whilst maintaining the joy in new discoveries. This enhances your own appreciation and joy. This may be in your own family life, or in a wider context. You will find that you understand the restlessness in people who have lost their direction and so you will be able to help them realise their hopes and dreams.

Carrying the birth vibration of the birth day number six can often mean that you are meant to take on huge commitments. This can be daunting if you are not in harmony with your source self and can cause anxiety or even anger issues. This is sheer frustration. However, returning to your spiritual practices and becoming more aware of the source self that you are, will give you the strength and trust you need to step forward, knowing that you set this in place for yourself before your incarnation.

When you place your trust fully in your source self you are a spiritual force that sweeps through life uplifting and illuminating so many peoples' lives.

If your Birth Day Energy is the Number Seven

If your birth day energy is the number seven you will find that you have 'been there before' or 'done it before' with many of your experiences. You will find that memories of past lives come to you at times of challenges as well as at times of spiritual study.

Your clarity and understanding of many different challenges can be a wonderful service to others. You will often find that you are drawn to helping people with deep trauma in their lives.

However, when you are not in harmony with your source self you will find that the colour of life becomes dimmer and a constant sadness is with you; you will have a feeling of loss. Sometimes you will look to others, feeling that you can find happiness through another, but it is never enough.

The need to be part of Source and to find Heaven on Earth is inbuilt so strongly in you that when you are out of alignment you feel the lack of source awareness more keenly than most.

If it is part of your soul journey to write, you will be inspired to write 'self help' books or media blogs, often with a new twist, which will come from your own experiences.

The media will often attract you, as you will have a need to teach and inspire, which could be the start of a life coaching career.

In a work place your light shines so brightly that you help people by just being close to them. Often a few inspired words can change a colleague's day for the better.

Be aware of days when you are feeling challenged as you could feel drained by others' fears and anxieties. It is very important, when challenges raise their heads that you are completely protected, grounded and connected to Source.

Family life can feel the same and sometimes you will wonder why you feel drained but your strong connection to Source can bring you back into alignment by merely using the power of posture and source breath. The affinity that you have with source breath will often lead you to classes that use the power of breath, like yoga.

Those that have the vibration of the number seven around them and the humbleness of their self worth, can inspire people to change their lives. You can do this from a stage, or one to one, with equal enthusiasm and love.

You have a magical way of showing others how a challenge or fear can be a gift from Source.

You will often be called a mentor and will change peoples' lives!

If your Birth Day Energy is the Number Eight

You will find that balance is essential in your life. You are very sensitive to disharmony, which makes maintaining a higher vibrational energy essential when you are around others' negativity.

You are also sensitive to many foods and additives. When your physical body is in harmony you are full of energy and can achieve huge amounts.

You are a planner and doer, you do what you say you will with integrity, which is a strong part of your vibration. You love people and will be the first one to stop and help others. Many people who carry the birth vibration of the birth date number eight will be people working within emergency situations, helping distressed and traumatised people.

You will want to save the world in every sense and if you are out of harmony this becomes a deeply personal commitment, which can interfere with your home and family life. When you are balanced you are able to detach but still feel huge compassion and love and you are a true light of salvation.

Your ability, from a balanced stable grounding, to manifest and create beauty and peace around people is incomparable. People will feel safe and secure around you. Many birth energy eight personalities make enlightened leaders in their need to better others' lives.

If you are not helping your fellow beings then it may be that your passion is in helping the planet. Mother Earth is now fourth density and as such is now calling many people to her aid. This is where one often finds the vibration of the number eight.

There is an army of enlightened beings throughout the world helping our beloved Mother Earth with the climate change chaos and anything else that is offensive to her wellbeing. You may find that with having a birth day of eight you are drawn towards these causes.

Your love of Mother Earth and her beauty will often draw you to spend as much time as you can in exploring all of her hidden beauties. This in turn will inspire you to do all you can to find solutions to help others in being aware of the harm that we inflict on her body.

It is in the growing understanding that we are all connected that inspires you to hold out the torch of love and light to your beloved fellow beings and Mother Earth.

If your Birth Day Energy is the Number Nine

When your birth day energy is the number nine, you are likely to be an old soul who has chosen to come back and help mankind. This does not mean that your challenges are any less, but they will be on a more spiritual level.

You may struggle with living in the material world and you may not always understand others' obsession with worldly goods as they are only a means to an end for you.

With this vibration you will be drawn to pilgrimages or special spiritual journeys of discovery, where huge amounts of wisdom are downloaded. You are often drawn to run spiritual retreats and help others towards enlightenment, which can be a life commitment.

With this vibration you may be drawn to religious orders, often in preparation for the spreading of huge amounts of light in a non-religious but spiritual way.

You are happiest when you are in service, especially to children, who need teachers who are aware of Source, or teaching people who have become aware of their source selves and need further guidance.

Some birth day energy number nine personalities are in a position of huge responsibility; these are old souls.

There are now more birth day energy number nine personalities in schools and influential positions than ever before. They are helping to plan the infrastructures for the greater good of mankind, and a more enlightened society.

In politics or business these number nine personalities need to be constantly grounded and connected. If this is you, then your huge energy and charisma will often sway decisions, big and small, in the correct and balanced way. This is a huge responsibility, where spiritual balance and protection are needed, otherwise physical or mental problems can result.

The number nine carries the vibration of the reflection of your own highest self, which can enable you to be aware, with great ease, of your connection to Source.

It is the awakened and spiritually aware birth day number nine personalities that can make huge changes in our world and are often leaders in many fields.

If you are reading this with a birth day energy of nine and you are unsure of where you are going, then stop and look at what you are doing at this very moment.

Call in your own source light and know that you are on your own soul journey.

If your Birth Day Energy is the Number Eleven

You are in service to Source and your soul journey is about changing lives. This vibration will fill you with a constant need to help and bring others to the awakened state of Christ Consciousness and Source Awareness.

Many of you will find that your soul journey is about overcoming huge and often devastating challenges, which will in the future enable you to help others with intuitive compassion and love.

Your ability to help others is because you usually see without illusion and are free from judgement. This enables you to see past the ego personality of others and instead see the shining being within.

You will, if called upon, make a great leader harnessing the expertise gained through your challenges. You exude love and integrity and bring out the best in others.

Some of you may be overwhelmed by your challenges and feel unable to complete your planned soul journey. This occurs when the ego personality is not in harmony with the source self; however, at these times your spirit guides will help you in many wondrous ways to give you the strength and resilience to continue although often the challenge is to see and understand the help and guidance.

It may be an idea to look at your life and remember the times when you perhaps felt this way and see from freshly opened eyes how you were helped.

You will often be drawn towards teaching, writing or becoming an inspirational leader, all ways in which to serve and help others. Often from a young age you will know that you have a huge commitment to others in service, this can make you feel rather separate from your school friends.

If you are reading this and feel overwhelmed, remember that having a birth day vibration of the number eleven is a gift of love, as it allows you to experience, in full, unconditional love and all that this means.

You will also be more aware than others that this is Divine Will, or in other words, your soul pathway to enlightenment. Your spiritual guides will be many and your connection to the wisdom of the universe will be strong. Your own mastery in all lives, past and future and in many dimensions is within you waiting to be called upon.

Often you will find that your source self will prompt you to take up the reins of many lifetimes experiences and you will be aware of the huge soul commitment, this is where being in a place free of fear and illusion is paramount and your constant daily grounding, connecting and protecting is a way of life.

It can be said that you walk in constant Source Awareness.

Method Five: How your Name Supports your Individual Soul Journey

Names

Every name is a vibrational song that is filled with 'the melody of Source'. Each time you change your name through marriage or choice you change the tune. When you say your name or you claim the power of 'I am'. For example "I am Penny", calls in the energy of the power animal and the sacred shape that is associated with the soul journey number of your name.

You will find that whether you are being casual by just using your first name, or you use your first and last names, you will draw towards you the appropriate power animal's source filled energy to help you be the highest and most effective 'being of light'.

The vibrational melody of your name will also attract the corresponding sacred shape around you. You only need to become aware of the source filled shape to feel the help and guidance this shape will bring to you. This is why it is important to know as much about a particular shape as you can through reading and even meditating for your own insights.

When people say your name they will surround your name with a small amount of their energy. If they surround your name with love or kindness, you will both feel it. Alternatively, if they surround your name with anger or fear then this is when the source filled power animal's energy helps you by making sure the vibrational tune of your name is surrounded with Divine Love. Simultaneously the source filled shape acts as a shield of Divine Light around you.

Your name is both a song of light and love but also draws towards you everything you need to stand in your Divine Love, withstanding those who are lost in their darkness, not able to recognise their light or yours.

The more you understand the power of your own melody and how you can use it to help you navigate your existence on Mother Earth, the more you will communicate from your source self.

When you say another's name remember you are rejoicing in their source melody. Choose to say their name with kindness and love.

Before birth, when you chose the source filled melody of your name you would have known the corresponding power animals and how they would help you through the density (challenges) of living on planet Earth by helping you to express your source self even in the most challenging of situations.

Remember your name is uniquely yours, constantly connecting you to the orchestra of the universe. Feel how you play your part in this vibrational symphony each time you say your name. It is the combination of the melody of your voice and the tune of your name that is your own source filled signature.

This way of working with letters is very straightforward. Each letter of the alphabet is associated with a number, as shown

1	2	3	4	5	6	7	8	9	11
A	B	C	D	E	F	G	H	I	J
K	L	M	N	O	P	Q	R	S	T
U	V	W	X	Y	Z				

We have looked at how the day that we were born gives us valuable insights into our soul journey and also our soul contract. The name that we use is how we are helping ourselves on our unique life journey to fulfil our soul contract.

For this we need to look at the name that we are known by, which is not necessarily the name on our birth certificate. For instance, my birth certificate gives my name as Jillian, but when I was a child I was known as Jill at school and Jillian at home, or even Jilly by some close friends. Then twenty plus years ago I woke up one morning and knew that I needed to be known as Jillian, the name I was given when I was born. This has made a huge difference to my soul journey and achieving my soul contract; so many opportunities, inspirations and great downloads have occurred within this last twenty plus years. Moving to a new home in 2022 I am now using the name Jilly, which feels appropriate at this time.

Your name is a constant reminder of why you are here. Every time your name is spoken you are attracting the purest vibration of that number towards you. The sound of your name activates the perfect vibration around you. An analogy would be, the front doorbell ringing, prompting you to take action.

Our name is more than our identification; it is a name that has been chosen to remind us during our life journey of why we are here. It carries the memory of everything we are meant to do, those activities that help us to clear the karma, learn the lessons and absorb the insights and gifts. All of this is part of our individual evolvement towards oneness with Source.

Look At the Name You are Known By

Look at the name you were given when you were born (this is the name on your birth certificate, not necessarily the name you were known by when you were a child).

Write the name down and underneath each letter write the number that corresponds with that letter, for example:

J	I	L	L	I	A	N
11	9	2	2	9	1	4

Then add up all the numbers that you have written under the letters:

$$11 + 9 + 2 + 2 + 9 + 1 + 4 = 38$$

As this number is still more than 11, then add these two numbers together:

$$3 + 8 = 11$$

Therefore, the soul journey number for the name Jillian is eleven.

However, Jillian may have been called Jill or Jilly as a child, which will have a different soul journey number:

J	I	L	L
11	9	2	2

J	I	L	L	Y
11	9	2	2	5

Add up the numbers you have under the letters of the name Jill:

$$11 + 9 + 2 + 2 = 24$$

Then add these two numbers together (as they are more than eleven):

$$2 + 4 = 6$$

Therefore, the soul journey number for the name Jill is six.

The name Jilly, adds up this way:

$$11 + 9 + 2 + 2 + 5 = 29$$

Then add the 2 and 9 together

$$2 + 9 = 11$$

Therefore, if Jillian was called by her full name, she was working with the vibration of the number eleven. If her name is shortened to Jilly she is also working with the eleven vibration. However, if the name she was known by is Jill then she was working with the vibration of the number six.

Lets look at another example

Take the name Patrick

P	A	T	R	I	C	K
6	1	11	8	9	3	1

Then add up all the numbers that you have written under the letters:

6 + 1 + 11 + 8 + 9 + 3 + 1 = 39

Add these two numbers together:

3 + 9 = 12 then

1 + 2 = 3

Therefore, the soul journey number for Patrick is three

However, if we look at the shortened form as Pat

P   A   T

6   1   11

Then, we add these three numbers together:

6 + 1 + 11 = 18

Add these two numbers together

1 + 8 = 9

Therefore, the soul journey number for Pat is nine.

If Patrick is known as Patrick, then he is working with the number three, but if he is known as Pat, then he is working with the number nine, so two different energies depending on the name that he is known by.

Looking at a third example, let us look at the name Daniel

D	A	N	I	E	L
4	1	4	9	5	2

Then add up all the numbers that you have written under the letters of Daniel:

4 + 1 + 4 + 9 + 5 + 2 = 25

Add these two numbers together:

2 + 5 = 7

Therefore, the soul journey number for Daniel is seven

However, Daniel may shorten his name to Dan, which will give a different vibration.

D	A	N
4	1	4

Then add up these numbers:

4 + 1 + 4 = 9

Therefore, the soul journey number for the name Dan is nine

Or, he may also be known as Danny

D	A	N	N	Y
4	1	4	4	5

Then add up these numbers:

4 + 1 + 4 + 4 + 5 = 18   1 + 8 = 9

Therefore, the soul journey number for the name Danny is also nine.

Daniel will therefore have different energies helping him on his own unique soul journey to achieve his soul contract depending on the name that he is using at that time. If he is known as Daniel then he will be working with the number seven and if he is known as either Dan or Danny, then he will be working with the number nine to help him achieve his soul contract on his soul journey.

Therefore, look closely at the name on your birth certificate and also the names you have been known by during your life. Remember this is the name you are known by (not including your given, other names or surname). *Are these numbers similar? Can you see the pattern that they are showing you?*

The name that you are known by influences how you are progressing on your own soul journey to achieve your soul contract. Does this influence the name that you wish to be known by?

We suggest that you give this careful consideration. The name that you are known by has such a huge effect on the progress that you can make in this lifetime. We need all the help we can get to move forward as easily as possible on our soul journey to achieve our soul contract.

Summary of How to use your Name to Support Yourself

There are several ways in which you can support yourself now that you know the soul journey number for your name.

One way to support yourself, is to use nature's own sacred geometric shapes. Look at the soul journey number for your name and see the shape associated with that number. The shape is a sacred safe space that helps you to find 'who you are', to 'feel who you are', it helps you to know yourself without the clamour of the ego.

Use one or more of the following to help and support you on your journey

> *Look at the image for the number for your name*

>> *What does this image mean to you?*

> *Look at the sacred shape for that image, and sit within that shape*

>> *If possible, sit within the shape for about 30 minutes*

>> *You will find that the echo of this sacred shape stays around you continually working with the vibration of your name, helping you to move forward*

>> *We suggest that you do this for seven days.*

For further insights you can use the pattern of the whole number, which are the two digits that are added together to get the number for your name.

Looking at the Core Resonance of your Name

If we have used more than one version of our name, for instance my name is either Jillian, Jill or Jilly, there is a core resonance within my name which is Jill, as these letters appear together in all versions of the names that I use.

Therefore, for an even deeper look at my name, and my life, I can look at Jill which adds up to 11+9+2+2=24. So, looking at the number six can be very helpful to me. The focus here is parent child relationship, which has been very important for me throughout my life. This gives extra clarity to this lifetime and the resonance that I am working with.

Another example would be Les, whose full name is Leslé. Adding up the numbers for Les we get 2+5+9=16 so seven, and Leslé, which is 2+5+9+2+5=23, so five. The core resonance of her name is Les, which is 2+5+9=16, so seven.

Therefore, whether Les is using Leslé or Les, she is working with the core resonance of seven, which she is also working with when she uses the name Les. This is actually the name she has always been known by. Attention to the breath is very important to her throughout this lifetime, as it is the resonance that she has chosen to work with for this incarnation.

Number One Intuitive Inspirations

The vibration of the number one helps you to feel complete, to know that you do not need anything from anyone else to feel at perfect ease, to feel whole.

It is the recognition of your source self. It can be the beginning of a phase or a new idea. It may be your source self prompting you with the vibration of number one to move forward into a new chapter of your soul journey.

When you draw the number one towards you, it is often because there are big events, or even major happenings, that you may feel apprehensive about.

You may be making excuses not to take an action or make a choice. These excuses in your fearful material world feel like very real reasons not to take the leap.

This is a time when it is very important to understand that the vibration of the number one is nudging you to spend even more time grounding, connecting and keeping yourself as pure as possible in order to detach from fear, thus enabling you to see clearly what is an excuse and what is reality.

This will help you to make the right decisions, whether it is finding the correct job, moving house, even changing your partner or choosing a partner that is perfectly right for you. Embracing the vibration of the number one will enable you to experience the wholeness of being in alignment with Divine Will.

Try these actions

As it is a time of new beginnings or perhaps a new thought or idea that you have been playing with for a while, take a moment to sit somewhere where you will not be disturbed and write down what has been coming into your mind.

Everything starts with a thought, and a good process is to take a small single step in that direction. An example would be that perhaps you have been wondering about joining a yoga class, so today would be a good day to encourage that thought. Let your mind play with that thought, think how good it would be to stretch your muscles, to use your breath in a powerful way. So a small step would be to locate a local yoga class, perhaps an online class. Just taking this step moves you forward and opens the door to perhaps an exciting new time in your life.

Give yourself space to allow a thought or an idea to emerge and blossom, this has the powerful assistance of the vibration of one.

Give yourself the gift of quiet space and time. You could choose to sit in a sphere of light or even move forward with the intention of keeping the sacred sphere of light around you, encouraging the growth of moving forward whilst being aware of the infinite possibilities that life has for you.

Number Two Intuitive Inspirations

The vibration of the number two will enable you to see both sides of a situation. The number two will help you to look at all relationships in your life, whether they are work related, your relationship with your partner or relationships with friends and colleagues. This number will help you to work with your personality self. This in itself is a lifelong challenge. However, when you are surrounded by the vibration of the number two certain blocks or painful memories will raise their heads and may stop you from connecting to your source self in a clear way.

The vibration of the number two is at its strongest when you are living in the present and are grounded. It may be time to look at some of your relationships and reassess them. These may be friendships, work relationships, partners, or even your role as a parent. The vibration of this number will bring a higher understanding of how to deal with these relationships from a detached, non-judgemental point of view that is free from neediness.

When you are drawn to the vibration of the number two, it is often your source self prompting you to face your relationships from a source perspective. Call on the Light of Source within you to help you find the courage, Divine strength and balance that you need to move forward. Ask the light of Source to help you love unconditionally and to see all your relationships from a compassionate, empathetic point of view.

Try these actions

One of the easiest ways to start this process is to find a space that fills you with a sense of peace. Perhaps a room in your house, or your garden, maybe a nearby park. It is your serious intention to deal with a relationship from a higher perspective that is needed and asking questions in a quiet space will allow you to connect with your source self. It is a good idea to write down your feelings and emotions surrounding the relationship as it helps the mind to calm, and you to look at your emotions from a detached place. Look at the emotions and feelings. Which one jumps out at you? Study it as you would if it was someone else who you are trying to help.

Perhaps, as an example, the emotion that really affects you is lack of control, a feeling of powerlessness. Are there other relationships in your life that make you feel the same way. Sit quietly and allow your mind to go to the first time you can remember this happening in the past. If this is the first time allow yourself to remember the first time the relationship made you feel powerless. To help you to understand why and what further boundaries you may need in future, it is a good idea to imagine yourself in the centre of a vesica piscis, the intersection of two overlapping spheres, each centred on the perimeter of the other, this helps you to enfold yourself in the powerful energy of number two. This is an ongoing process and see it as a lesson in understanding and how to take steps to take control of your life and put boundaries in place so that you can move forward in a positive and constructive way to facing your relationships.

Number Three Intuitive Inspirations

The vibration of the number three is an understanding of Christ Consciousness.

When you are drawn to the vibration of the number three it often means a deep soul yearning for a stronger awareness of your own Christ Consciousness.

It also brings a deeper understanding of the Trinity, and the fact that there is Trinity in all aspects of your life.

Whatever you are dealing with, there is always a third higher vibration present. We have the energy of our ego personality, our source self and Source. The vibration of three will remind you to connect strongly with your source self.

The vibration of the number three will prompt you to connect to your higher wisdom, your own deep inner wisdom and the mastery that you have achieved in past lives.

If you are surrounded by the vibration of the number three, it will help you to connect with your higher intuition, especially if you are doing guidance sessions for other people.

Use your source breath to connect consciously to your source self:

> *To help you to recognise your own wisdom as well as the wisdom in others. To help you to recognise the difference between your higher intuition and your ego personality.*

Try these actions

Find a quiet secluded space and with intention, take some source filled breaths.

To do this, you could place your hand over your heart (this helps to bring attention to your heart). Now imagine you are breathing in through your heart. Breathe in for the slow count of four and then slowly breathe out to the same count of four.

Do this again, this time as you breathe out feel as though you are letting go of all tension and anxiety.

Now try this again and as you breathe in imagine the air has in it everything you need, happiness, joy, wisdom, peace, everything that is Source. Let your breathing become a rhythm that is perfect for you. Know that you are breathing in source filled air and letting go of everything that stops you from being the true wise loving person that you are.

Number Four Intuitive Inspirations

The energy of the number four holds the vibration of steadfastness and stability. When you call for the vibration of the number four to surround you it will help you to bring Heaven to Earth, connecting and grounding you.

As a spiritual being the number four helps you to identify the difference between reality and illusion. This is very helpful when making decisions or choices.

When you are constantly working at a spiritual level, such as healing, then the vibration of the number four will help you to stay focused and be more aware of the messages that you receive from the masters.

The number four helps you to balance your emotions and thoughts in a more positive way, and to understand why you have thoughts and emotions that are not for your highest good. If you need to bring balance and flow into your physical world, by decluttering or reorganising your home or workspace, then you will attract the vibration of the number four.

This may also be the time to examine relationships and focus on whether they are balanced and harmonious. The vibration of the number four helps you to do this in a grounded way, uncluttered by thoughts and emotions of neediness. Use your source breath to connect consciously to your source self: this will help you to find the courage and integrity to face and deal with any disharmony within your life. This will help you to review your challenges from a Christ Conscious perspective.

Try these actions

Find a place out in nature, or if that is not possible, near a picture or image that helps you to imagine yourself outside surrounded by nature. Use your breath and intention to connect to Mother Earth. This will help you to harmonise your body and mind and feel grounded and connected to the life force that is within you and all around you. This is extremely liberating and freeing.

Take some soft breaths all the while focusing on your breathing. As you are doing this become aware of the sounds of nature around you, real or imagined.

Feel yourself becoming part of nature. If it helps, focus on a flower, a plant or anything you find beautiful, real or imagined.

Feel as if you are breathing with this part of nature, that you are nature. Now raise your eyes upwards to the sky and breathe in the energy of the sky, the clouds and finally the sun. You are a bridge between Heaven and Earth. You are connected to Heaven and Earth. Do this until it feels as if you are one with all. Now walk the rest of your day with the intention of seeing everything and everyone as part of you. This will help you to stay positive and see the reality of situations in a loving uncluttered manner. If you want to have an uncluttered space, be it at home or at work then having this strong grounded connection with Source will help you to achieve this.

Number Five Intuitive Inspirations

The number five is about breaking free from ties that bind you.

The number five carries the vibration of Divine Will whilst allowing you free will. If you are called upon to work within the vibration of the number five it will mean that you are being asked to look at what is holding you back, in both your physical life and your spiritual life.

Are you holding yourself back with self made ties of guilt and perhaps unwarranted responsibilities?

If you feel the number five around you then look at your life with eyes filled with clarity. It will be time to release old hurts and blockages with deep honesty, so that you become free from karma that has been causing you to stumble in this life.

The number five also carries a habit of great strength to enable you to overcome your personality self and move forward as a Being of Source. So understand that you can do all that your soul requires for soul growth.

Use your source breath to connect consciously to your source self:

> *To see with clarity and vision what it is that you need to change.*
> *To help you acknowledge your full self worth.*

Try these actions

Use your breath as a tool to help you to surrender to your source self. In order to let go of what is binding you, you need to understand what it is that stops you from surrendering. Before you start it is important to understand that resistance is fear.

Fear can be released when it is faced. Fear is shown in many ways. Anger and loneliness are two very strong projections of fear. Find a quiet place where you will be undisturbed and allow your mind to show you your closest fear. Be aware that the ego self can hide your most damaging fear so sit with it and allow your intuition to take you further into your innate knowing. Accept what you feel.

To help feel safe and filled with source light, imagine you are sitting in a four sided pyramid with a square base. This will keep you grounded but allow you to connect strongly with Source. Now see your fear filled emotion or thought outside your light filled sacred pyramid.

Say your fear out loud. Listen to yourself admitting to your fear. It is out there and you, the source being that you are, are sitting inside your sacred shape. You can see it is not you. It has no power over you.

Now use your slow four count breath to dissolve it, to let go. Surrender to the light that is within you, the light that is filled with Divine Will, you are free will to be what you are meant to be. Take your time, be loving in allowing yourself to spend time enjoying the process of surrendering through your source breath.

Number Six Intutive Inspirations

When you have the vibration of the number six around you, it will often mean that your higher consciousness is communicating, so make time to stop and listen. Allow the Christ conscious vibration of the number six to prompt you; look at the choices and challenges in your life from the perspective of your source self. The vibration of the number six often reveals our blockages. As this number is so closely linked with the Trinity of 'all that is', you will find that the solutions or answers to your challenges will arrive easily and with synchronicity.

The vibration of the number six will also help you to notice the synchronicity of events and their deeper meanings. You will often resonate with this vibration of the number six when you are being led towards further study or teaching. It is a vibration that is filled with Divine Wisdom. This vibration will encourage you to take that leap of faith. Often when you call for, or are attracted to, this vibration, it may mean that there are blocks stopping you from seeing what others see and expect from you, and that your lack of self worth is being shown as a lack of confidence. Perhaps it is time to ask yourself whether your lack of confidence is actually fear based or a result of low self esteem? The vibration of the number six will help you to reach your inner heart wisdom

Use your Source breath to connect consciously to your Source self:

To help you to connect to your own wisdom.
To help you to become a confident teacher, when the need arises.
To help you to see your true self worth and have the confidence to reach for your dreams.

Try these actions

Now is the time to face your dreams, the dreams that are waiting for you to claim. First you need to face the blockages that you, and maybe others, are putting in your soul pathway. Go to your favourite quiet space and make sure you will be undisturbed for at least 40 minutes. Now start your own gentle rhythm of source breath. Remember all breath is source filled but your intention and awareness makes your connection even stronger.

Breathe from your heart and after a few breaths, use your intention to breathe a light filled diamond of light around you. This sacred shape is an octahedron. This embodies sacred love, the Divine Feminine. Sit quietly in your own soft rhythm of breath until the diamond of light feels strong around you. With each breath you are allowing yourself to see the magnificent being that you are, filled with the confidence of knowing that you can reach for your dreams. The more you focus and give energy and thus life to a particular dream, the more the blockages fade away. They lose their power through the lack of your focus. A powerful way of using the octahedron, the diamond of light, is to have the intention of walking with it around you throughout your day. During the day, whenever it comes into your mind, use a couple of breaths to settle it around you. This will draw synchronistic events towards you and give you the confidence and wisdom to make soul driven choices. This is what makes a dream into a possibility and then a reality.

Number Seven Intuitive Inspirations

The number seven is the breath of Source.

When you have the vibration of number seven around you, you are being encouraged to use conscious source breath. Work on re aligning with Source through your posture and breath. The energy of the number seven helps you to connect to your source self and also helps your connection to others. This is very strong when you are giving guidance or a healing.

Be aware that when you attract the vibration of the number seven it may be that there are blockages and karma to be dealt with from the perspective of your source self. Similarly, you will often attract the vibration of the number seven when you are healing and your client has karma that needs to be cleared. The vibration of the number seven can be inspirational and if you are in the midst of a new venture or idea allow the vibration of the number seven to release the creativity within you.

The vibration of the number seven is often needed around you to open your eyes to an idea that is totally out of your comfort zone, the sort of idea that perhaps you have thought about but never felt that you could manage. If the idea makes your heart race a little with excitement and delight then sit in the vibration of number seven with the help of the light of Source and feel inspired. All great deeds come from an inspired thought!

Use your Source breath to connect consciously to your Source self:

To help you to make that strong connection to your creativity of Divine Love.
To help you find the deep integrity and connectedness you need to bring you back to alignment with Source.
To help you to connect to your higher intuition at times when you are life coaching.

Try these actions

Remember that the breath of Source is seven. When you have that intention to use your source breath you will activate the energy of seven around you. Knowing this, use your intention with uninterrupted focus. Find a quiet space. If you can, go outside to a secluded spot, if that is not possible then near an open window.

As you start your own perfect rhythm of source breath, remember that each breath carries source possibilities. Each breath is a promise of creation. With intention and using your source breath, breathe yourself into the centre of seven interlocking spheres. You are the seed of life. From here comes healing and all possibilities. Once you have your sacred space around you start your source breath. Breathe in to your heart for the count of four, pause and gently breathe out to the count of four, pause and start again. This must be at your own gentle pace. What you need to concentrate on is the pause between the in and out breath. The pause is you touching the infinite. The all that is. The pause is timeless and a remembering of everything that has been or will be. This is the power of seven. Spend 10 minutes twice a day doing this with the intention of being in perfect alignment with Source.

Number Eight Intuitive Inspirations

If the vibration of the number eight surrounds you it will often mean that you need to look at the origins of your creating and manifesting. In other words, if you want to create a change in your life or manifest a loving relationship and it does not feel as if it is happening, it is time to look at what could be blocking you, from a balanced and pure perspective. Perhaps there are blocks or karma relating to poverty or lack that could go back to your early life or even past lives.

The vibration of the number eight will encourage you to access your deep intuition more easily, and so find the answers that are already within your own inner wisdom. It is a time to be deeply honest with yourself.

The vibration of the number eight allows the concept of cause and effect to be seen in day to day challenges. This helps you to understand why certain situations or phases keep repeating or happening to you. You will often find the vibration of the number eight will surround you when you are drawn to do energy healing. It carries a strong heart to heart vibration that allows empathy for the client to flow freely.

Use your source breath to connect consciously to your source self:

> *To help you with a heart to heart connection to others and to bring more awareness and understanding of the more subtle blocks that you or your client might have.*

> *To help you to purify and balance your emotions and thoughts in order to connect to your source self and thus achieve the clarity that is needed to understand the lack of harmony and the blocks that are preventing the manifestation of your dreams.*

Try these actions

Now is the time you manifest with positive intent. This is as powerful as you want it to be. See clearly what it is that you want. Use your source filled breath to help you focus on why you want whatever it is that you desire. This is important as the reason why you want something may be surrounded by fear fuelled emotions. This in turn could block your manifesting.

Find a quiet place where you will be undisturbed. Ground and connect yourself into the present moment by focusing on your own rhythm of source breath. It is by being present that you will find the real reason why you want to manifest something. Breathe around you the six pointed star, the star tetrahedron. You may want to call in the energy of the red admiral butterfly to be with you. From this space imagine the feeling of joy you would have if you achieved what it is you truly want. The energy of the star tetrahedron will help you to come to the truth of your desire and know whether it is meant for you on your soul journey. Allow time for this and perhaps spend the day surrounded by the energy of the sacred star with the transformational butterfly to help you find out what your soul desires, free from fear, and perfectly right for your soul growth and expansion.

Number Nine Intuitive Inspirations

When you have, or call in, the vibration of the number nine around you, you will be completely in touch with your Christ Conscious self. Your inner awareness of your Christ self will colour and affect all you do. When you work with the sphere of light your ability to use it in more ways than just protection will be more accessible and understood. Take time to use the sphere of light as a mirror of your own deeply mastered wisdom.

Ask a question and allow yourself to relax into a place of peace; have no expectations but know that everything is as it is meant to be. You will find that pure guidance flows through you without being tainted by fear or your personality self and your guidance will be filled with the integrity of Source.

You are often drawn to re-evaluate your life and the vibration of the number nine will help you to see where spiritual balance is needed. This is often when your source self is prompting you to higher service, which can be daunting; remember that you would not be asked if you were not ready for this service.

Use your source breath to connect consciously to your source self:

To help you to connect with your source self and have the confidence to step forward on your soul journey.

To help you to connect to your inner peace, allowing you to feel your Christ Conscious self in a more profound and fulfilling way.

Try these actions

You are called to connect to your Christ Conscious self with a light filled intention. A good way of doing this is to focus on your heart and the energy surrounding it. Find a place that fills your heart with joy. In a garden, in your favourite chair, even looking at a view that makes your heart swell with a positive emotion.

Give yourself the gift of an undisturbed 40 minutes. Place your hands over your heart and feel as if you are breathing your source filled breath through your heart. To help this, imagine you are surrounded by a rainbow coloured sphere of light. Within the sphere is a diamond shape of golden white light. As you breathe it in let this light enfold you, and feel yourself being infused with golden white light. With each gentle source breath you become brighter and brighter. You are brighter than the sun. This light is love from your heart. Allow the light to expand outwards, simultaneously feel the peace of this love fill you, every cell in your body.

When you are ready allow your source self to bring to you the guidance you need for whatever life situation is presenting itself to you. You are ready to listen. You just have to believe it, to trust in the Christ within. Once you have mastered the gentle art of breathing through your heart in the rhythm that is perfect for you, you will be able to use this technique at any time of the day or night to centre yourself and find the deep peace that is the Christ Consciousness within.

Number Eleven Intuitive Inspirations

The number eleven is a powerful and profound vibration, which helps you to be present and well grounded at all times. This is about the bliss of recognising the Source within. The number eleven is an intensely healing vibration and is very beneficial when you are doing energy work.

When you attract the number eleven and you are involved in energy healing, you will find that your healing will often contain soul lessons for you, as well as your client. To avoid the confusion during the healing, ensure that you are not affected in any way by the client's problems. In other words remain detached whilst allowing your empathy and compassion to flow.

This is not always easy to do and you will find that the vibration of the number eleven and guidance from your source light will help you. You will often be drawn to the vibration of the number eleven when you are dealing with karmic issues. This allows you to have clear vision from your source self which increases your understanding.

The energy of number eleven is a wonderful energy to have around you when you are in a spiritual relationship with others, like teaching or coaching. You will find that your connection to Source and understanding of 'all that is' is profound.

Use your source breath to connect consciously to Source.

To help you to stay present and grounded at all times.
For guidance whilst teaching and also for strengthening your connection to Divine Will.

Try these actions

Now is the time to shine with the light of who you really are. So often you have clouds obscuring your true sun or source self. The clouds are barriers made of illusions and fearful thoughts. When you choose an image that has the energy of eleven, you draw the energy of the snow leopard towards you. You only have to say 'yes' to its energy and you will find your true self is given free rein. The authenticity of what you are will shine from you. Your fearlessness allows you to speak to and work with others from a place of love and quiet wisdom.

As well as keeping the snow leopard at your side you may want to use your source breath to breathe a twelve pointed star around you. Feel how this releases your imagined fears and shows you a life situation from a higher perspective. Perhaps you can sit with the snow leopard curled up at your feet. Allow this power animal to show you what it is you really need, to help you to move forward in any life situation in a love filled compassionate manner. Remember the number eleven is with you to to remind you that there are new beginnings close by. These promptings will be your soul gently guiding you to start your day or a new challenge or a new idea from the Divine Will within. Surrender to your source self today and allow the day to flow.

Method Six: Further Insights using Month and Year Numbers

This helps us to work out the predominant energy around us for a certain year or month. The year number is like an 'umbrella' for the year and each monthly image will help you to understand the energies of the year in more detail.

To calculate the Year Number

Add the number for the current year to the total of your full birthdate number. For instance: someone born with the birthdate number of nine and if the year is 2024. So we add all the numbers together and we get 17, which gives us the year soul journey number of eight for this person. Use all the images for the number eight to help understand where the year is taking you, plus the intuitive inspirations for number eight on page 108.

To calculate the Month Number

Add the number of the current month, so June will be six, added to the year 2024, plus your full birthdate number, say nine from our previous example,

Giving $6 + 2 + 0 + 2 + 4 + 9 = 23$ so $2 + 3 = 5$

Use the main number five image and the source energy pattern 5 (2+3) to gain insights into your month, plus the intuitive inspiration for number five on page 105.

Method Seven: Working with the Power Animals

The power animals play a significant role in all aspects of the images you have been working with. Method seven looks at the power animal relating to your name, particularly the core resonance of your name. Turn to the appropriate page relating to the power animal for the core resonance of your name, in my case, it is Jill and number six.

Notice the qualities and traits of the power animal as well as the challenging traits and situations, or the subtle echoes of them. Work with the power animal to work with the challenges to turn them into your gifts, enhancing all the positive qualities.

Method Eight: Working with the Sacred Shapes

There are six active awareness images, which contain the six sacred shapes. Ground, breathe and choose a sacred shape code from the list below, then turn to page 114, to see your chosen active awareness image. Turn to the appropriate page in the book between 115 and 127 read about the shape and work with it. At the end of the day take time to evaluate how the shape has helped you to overcome challenges or find solutions.

M3   Y1   D1   J2   N1   Y3

H1   J1   L2   W1   S1   T2

Method Nine: Working with Past Lives

There are two active awareness sacred shapes that help us to work with our past lives; these are the 'seed of life' and the 'twelve pointed star'.

The seed of life brings to you the seeds of the achievements and the gifts that you have learnt in your last past life, to help you in this life time. Whatever the gifts are, you bring them into this life, but they are just seeds. This sacred shape helps these seeds to grow and flourish in this life, so that the lessons that you have learnt are brought to the front, to help you with what you have to do in this life.

The twelve pointed star also helps you to integrate and learn from past lives. This shape is the main shape for working with the relevant past life. It is telling you that which you need to know in this lifetime. This is the starting point of what happened, how it relates to this lifetime and the happenings that require forgiveness. The active awareness image, the twelve pointed star will help and support you here.

These soul guidance images can also help you to understand past lives and bring forward the wisdom to use in this lifetime.

The power animal, the snow leopard, also helps you to understand and integrate the wisdom from past lives. The snow leopard is inter-dimensional, it can go forwards, backwards and up and down, and helps you to do the same. So this is an incredible shape shifting animal to work with.

We recommend that you work with the seed of life first, so that you know what you have brought with you into this life. You may like to work with the twelve pointed star as well in order to move forward towards enlightenment.

Method A Working with the Seed of Life

Sit quietly, where you will not be disturbed, take a few deep diaphragm breaths, and ensure you are well grounded and present in the moment.

Observe the seed of life active awareness image, to help you to connect with the seeds of the achievements and the gifts that you have learnt in your last past life, to help you in this lifetime.

Then look at the four images that relate to the number seven. Take some deep diaphragm breaths and ask for the appropriate image to help you with the gifts you are bringing forward from past lives. Intuitively select the appropriate number seven image. Look at the appropriate page in the book to understand more about your chosen image.

Close your eyes and surround yourself with the shape of the seed of life. Call in either the snow leopard or the dolphin to help and support you, be aware of your chosen source energy number seven image. Sit quietly absorbing the messages, insights and inspirations that are the gifts from your past life and be aware of how these may be integrated in to this life.

Be aware of how these seeds are growing and flourishing in this life to help you to move forward towards enlightenment, integrating the lessons that you have brought forward to help you with your soul journey in this lifetime.

In your own time, when you are ready, thank Source, Mother Earth, the seed of life, and the power animal for their help and support and bring your attention back into the room and feel yourself sitting comfortably on the chair, still well grounded and present in the moment and when you are ready open your eyes.

Method B Working with the Twelve Pointed Star

Sit quietly, where you will not be disturbed, take a few deep diaphragm breaths, and ensure you are well grounded and present in the moment.

Observe the twelve pointed star active awareness image, to help you to integrate and learn from past lives.

Take some deep diaphragm breaths, ensure that you are centered and grounded. Use the charts on pages 11 and 114 to choose the perfect image to help you integrate and learn from past lives. Study your image and absorb the energy, then look at the appropriate page in the book to understand more about your chosen image.

Close you eyes and surround yourself with the shape of the twelve pointed star. Call in the snow leopard to help and support you. Be aware of your chosen number image. Sit quietly absorbing the messages, insights and inspirations that your past life is helping you to integrate and learn. Be aware of how these insights, inspirations and knowings are being integrated to help and support you in this life, so helping you to move forward towards enlightenment, integrating the wisdom and knowledge that you have brought forward to help you on your soul journey in this lifetime.

In your own time, when you are ready, bring your attention back into the room, thank Source, Mother Earth, the twelve pointed star and the power animal for their help and support and and feel yourself sitting comfortably on the chair, still well grounded and present in the moment and when you are ready open your eyes.

Label	Value	Label	Value	Label	Value
A1	6 (2+4)	A2	6	A3	5 (2+3)
B1	1	B2	11 (3+8)	B3	8 (2+6)
C1	9 (1+8)	C2	6 (2+4)	C3	6 (3+3)
D1	Tet	D2	4	D3	11 (4+7)
E1	8 (3+5)	E2	9 (2+7)	E3	4 (1+3)
F1	5	F2	8	F3	11
G1	11 (3+8)	G2	5 (1+4)	G3	8 (4+4)
H1	Oct	H2	6 (1+5)	H3	1
I1	5 (2+3)	I2	8 (3+5)	I3	9 (4+5)
J1	Sph	J2	Pyr	J3	7 (3+4)
K1	11	K2	7 (3+4)	K3	9 (1+8)
L1	2	L2	Star	L3	3 (1+2)
M1	5 (1+4)	M2	8 (2+6)	M3	Tet
N1	Oct	N2	11 (2+9)	N3	2
O1	9	O2	6 (3+3)	O3	7
P1	7 (2+5)	P2	4	P3	7 (2+5)
Q1	8	Q2	9 (4+5)	Q3	5
R1	7	R2	11 (4+7)	R3	6 (1+5)
S1	Pyr	S2	4 (1+3)	S3	7 (1+6)
T1	3	T2	Seed	T3	11 (5+6)
U1	9 (2+7)	U2	8 (1+7)	U3	4 (2+2)
V1	11 (2+9)	V2	8 (4+4)	V3	3
W1	Seed	W2	3 (1+2)	W3	9 (3+6)
X1	4 (2+2)	X2	11 (5+6)	X3	6
Y1	Star	Y2	9	Y3	Sph
Z1	9 (3+6)	Z2	7 (1+6)	Z3	8 (1+7)

Sph = Sphere   Pyr = Pyramid   Octa = Octahedron
Tetra= Tetrahedron 12 Pointed Star   Seed = Seed of Life

ACTIVE AWARENESS

Introduction to Active Awareness Images

Active awareness is when we are able to sustain the state of being present, and fully in alignment with our source selves, in a conscious manner.

There are six active awareness images that help us to achieve this.

Each active awareness image carries the vibration of a sacred geometric shape which we are attracted to when the shape's vibration is perfectly right for us at a particular time or situation.

Being drawn towards a particular active awareness image enables us to use a sacred geometric shape that will help us to understand our deepest subconscious programming in a detached but aware manner.

The sacred shapes are individual universal signatures that act as enlightening channels enabling us to seek the greater wisdom of our source self.

Although each shape has a different vibrational signature each will resonate with our own particular needs. They all are about helping us on our source conscious journey.

These are two powerful ways to use these images:

Let yourself be led intuitively by your source self to which of these methods is perfect for you.

This takes practice as it is your intention and focus that makes this a powerful Source communication.

1. *You can use your imagination and see and feel the shape around you. Imagine that you are completely surrounded by the shape; see yourself touching the shape. Perhaps you can sense a colour or even a sound. Your senses are source filled indicators of what your source self wants you to do to experience the vibration of the shape.*

2. *You can use your breath to breathe the shape around you. This is an easy method to use if you acknowledge the power of breath; correct breathing is a direct connection to Source.*

As you breathe the shape around you, feel the Divine Love within your source breath creating the shape. You are accessing the creator within and without.

Try each of these methods and you may find that after practice you are able to combine these two methods.

This is active awareness that is to say, active intent with Divine Guidance.

ACTIVE AWARENESS
Sphere

ACTIVE
AWARENESS

SPHERE
You are called to work with this shape

The sphere is Divine, it has no beginning or ending. It is, in its simplicity, the perfect vibration for all that is.

If we are drawn to this image we are engaging in the part of us that responds to Source. In other words we are recognising our true selves.

In these images the sphere also presents itself in multiples, that is two interlocking spheres (vesica piscis), three interlocking spheres and seven interlocking spheres (seed of life). Each of these representations of the sphere has a different vibrational signature.

However, when we are drawn to the 'active awareness' sphere image, it is our soul calling to us to experience ourselves in our purest state.

This is our source self: the source being that is infinite.

When we understand that we are infinitely more than the temporary material body; that we are Source experiencing life through the limiting finite body, we will find it easier to express our life through the eyes of Source.

This simple but infinitely powerful shape is the womb for the creation of all wisdom and the ultimate expression of truth. If we are drawn to this image then we are being asked to understand that we are already universal wisdom and the truth of Source; however, we may not always see this and perhaps in our striving for enlightenment we may have lost our way.

Feeling lost is when there is no clarity about how to move forward. This can apply to many areas of our lives.

Active Awareness

Having drawn this image, we are being asked to look at our lives.

Consider these questions:

Am I confused by the chaos around me?

Do I wonder why situations happen that are not to my liking?

These can be seen as small unpleasant occurrences or life changing happenings that feel as if our world has been turned upside down.

This is a soul prompting that is encouraging us to reevaluate our lives.

However, this can be a major stumbling block for us as when we are in these situations as we are often in the survival mode (fight, flight, or freeze).

We switch to this mode whenever our ego/personality self feels threatened. This is fear, the polar opposite of love.

Ask yourself:

Do I feel guilty in this situation? (This can be seen as 'flight')

Do I blame someone or something else for this situation? (This can be seen as 'fight').

Do I feel overwhelmed? (This can be seen as 'freeze')

If we resonate with these questions then it will be helpful to use the following meditation to help us to understand that we are judging either ourselves or others. Judgement is a fearful reaction from our ego/personality self. We need to find the Divine Truth of the situation through our Divine Wisdom.

Active Awareness Action

Find a quiet place where you will be undisturbed. You may want to connect to the power animal the blue whale.

Take some deep source filled breaths, which will help you to be present. Become aware of the life force in each part of your body as you continue to take soft source filled breaths in a rhythm that is perfect for you.

Take your attention to that quiet sacred place within your heart and breathe into your awareness a sphere of light.

Feel it surround you with its signature vibration of universal truth. Feel yourself become an observer of the distressing situation you believe yourself to be in.

The vibrational energy of the sphere will help you to detach from the situation as you allow your source self to be an observer.

When you are fully connected to your source self and you view the situation through the eyes of Source, you cease to be a victim to circumstance. You are now in your own powerful truth.

Step into your own Divine Power.

Spend time in this source filled sacred geometric shape and allow the universal wisdom to fill you with understanding and insights that help you to move forward and see your life in a new light.

This will help you to move away from the judgement that guilt and blame brings.

Feel how the peace of your source self fills you and continue to walk your soul path in harmony. Bathe in the love and light of the sphere every day until you find yourself free from the pain of indecision.

ACTIVE AWARENESS
Pyramid

Four sided pyramid with a square base

This sacred source filled shape carries the vibration of the soul journey number five.

We as humans resonate strongly with the number five and will find that we can easily merge ourselves with the energy of this shape.

This is a shape that is found in many civilisations. Perhaps the most well known are the Egyptian pyramids. It is from this civilisation's records and legends that we find the many thoughts and beliefs connected to this shape.

The one steadfast belief is that the pyramid can be seen as a healing chamber and can be used to increase the healing process. The shape is also a symbolic representation of connecting the Earth with Heaven.

When you draw this image towards you, you are being asked to step away from the personality self and acknowledge that you are a combination of Heaven and Earth, or the Mother and Father Divine.

This shape vibrates with a frequency that will feel familiar as it carries the history of planetary life and also the ever expanding process of understanding that we are beings of pure Source experiencing life in a material body. This being the case, it is the perfect shape to enhance the physical body's own healing. It reflects, in a geometric shape, what we are, a combination of Source (Heaven) and material (Earth). This shape is about Source experiencing life in a material form; however, this is not always an easy concept to take on board.

Growth Awareness

If you draw this image towards you, you may need to ask yourself these questions:

How connected to Source do I feel?
How much time do I spend in gratitude for the fun and pleasure I have in my life?
To resonate on a deeper level ask yourself these three questions:
Do I feel constantly restless and anxious?
Do I worry about the future?
Do I sometimes feel listless or depressed?

Life can be all consuming and in order not to be submerged in the everyday challenges that may arise we need to be constantly aware that what we are experiencing, is in fact, not real; it is an experience through which our source self is experiencing itself. However, just because we know this does not make the health, financial or relationship issues feel any less challenging.

Meditating within the four sided pyramid amplifies this understanding as it helps us to detach from our anxieties and fears and we are able to observe, from a higher perspective, why we are drawing these challenging situations towards us.

Before you start meditating or using this shape, be very clear of its geometry. This means that when you visualise this shape around you, you are very clear about the shape you are working with.

Then, if you have identified with one of the questions above and, before you start, make sure you feel no resistance to the question and that you will be open to what you learn about yourself.

This allows your source self to connect by surrendering to just being, allowing the flow of Source through you.

The pyramid acts as a lighthouse beacon to show you your deepest limitations, allowing you to see clearly, free from fear.

Active Awareness Action

Find a quiet space where you will be undisturbed. Visualise a four sided pyramid around you. See it in your imagination and use your source filled breath to breathe life into it. You may want to call in the jaguar to help you. You may be drawn to the colours on the image.

One of the strongest connections to your source self is gratitude. Gratitude carries the vibration of the number one. With this in mind see your pyramid as five (1x5) different aspects of gratitude in your life. Once you have filled yourself with the positive emotion of gratitude it is easy to step into the role of being an observer.

Sit in this dynamic geometric space as an observer, see your physical body, feel how grateful you are for this creation.

See into your feelings, feel how at peace you are with the feelings and emotions that carry the light of truth.

See into your thoughts and notice how often you think uplifting, positive, fulfilling thoughts.

Once you have mastered the feeling of gratitude, allow any limitations to be shown to you.

As an observer, in other words, the source aspect of you, see the futility of the personality self's negativity. You will find you can let it go. This is done through understanding where the fear filled thoughts and subsequent fears come from.

This process starts a deep healing that is a journey in itself of soul discovery. Take time with this sacred shape and use it as often as you can.

You may want to surround yourself in the four sided pyramid as you go through your day. This is a wonderful way to help you walk your day in a state of being consciously aware.

ACTIVE AWARENESS
Octahedron

This source filled sacred geometric shape can also be described as a four sided pyramid with a square base and an identical inverted pyramid beneath it. This shape is also referred to as a diamond shape.

The signature or vibration of the octahedron is unconditional love, which can also be described as 'all that is'. This means that everything that is real is love and everything else is merely an illusion that our personality self has created.

When there is a feeling of lack, the emotions or feelings that we may call love will be infused with this lack, which in turn creates fear. This means that our love will have conditions and needs. In other words, unconditional love has no expectations, it just is.

As the purpose of life is to experience separateness in order to understand 'oneness' the journey to this understanding can produce fear and the feeling of lack. It can then be understood that the signature of this geometric shape may resonate with us many times in this lifetime.

It is through experiencing relationships that our biggest challenges of duality or separateness are experienced.

That is why, if we draw this image towards us, it may well mean that we need to scrutinise the relationships in our life.

Every interaction with another sentient being is a relationship. It is how we relate with each other that is a measure of soul growth.

Active Awareness

We have family relationships, work related relationships, partner and spouse relationships. We also have relationships with friends, groups of people, animals and also religions. This last factor may not be seen as a relationship but how we relate to a religion or a belief system can dominate our life choices and decisions.

The most important relationship is with our source self, the understanding that we are Source and that our personality self is a tool through which our source self can express itself.

The personality or ego self is a mindset created by our subconscious. This is a memory bank that chooses selective memories to keep us from perceived harm. It is not real.

How we see our relationships is often tainted by feelings and emotions that arise from this memory bank.

Take a moment to consider all the relationships in your life. Do your various relationships create harmony or disharmony in your life?

If you are finding that in certain relationships you are often in a place of disharmony your reactions may be because you feel on the defence. When you relate to a challenging situation within a relationship do you respond from a place of understanding or do you react from a place of resistance?

Perhaps you are dissatisfied with certain relationships and you are not sure how to change the dynamics of the relationship. The energy of this sacred shape will help you to see the perceived grievances from an objective point of view rather than your subjective reality.

The energy of the octahedron helps us to see our relationship challenges from our source self, the place of unconditional love.

Active Awareness Action

Find a quiet place where you feel at peace and in harmony with your surroundings. Concentrate on your breath, feel and hear your breath and with intention breathe in the light of Source. Feel how grounded and connected you feel. From this space visualise yourself in the centre of a glowing octahedron.

You may have a stronger feeling if you visualise the pure source light pouring out from your heart centre and filling the octahedron.

Sit in this highest signature of love, which is unconditional love.

Spend as much time as you need in this space feeling loved. Allow yourself to be filled with the emotion of self love. It is this loving of yourself that allows you to love others.

If you struggle with this then spend time in this shape, as it will help you to love parts of yourself that you find unlovable. More importantly it helps you to forgive those aspects, as they are merely projections of fear.

This is the key to being able to relate to others from a love filled heart so it is vital that you do not skip this step.

This is a wonderful healing process; however it may take time as it is like peeling an onion and the layers will be become more subtle and yet give greater insight on self love and self worth.

When you see yourself from a source filled perspective and feel unconditional love for yourself you are ready to look at your relationships.

ACTIVE AWARENESS
Star Tetrahedron

Consisting of two Tetrahedra

This sacred source filled shape carries the vibration of the soul journey number eight.

This shape is most commonly referred to as a star tetrahedron. It also known by other labels; a merkabah being one such label.

There are many definitions of what we may experience when we are working within this vibrational structure of Source; however, when we draw this image it indicates that we need balance in an aspect, or aspects, of our life.

This sacred shape is about balance. We need balance in our physical lives, in our physical, mental and emotional bodies and in our spiritual awakening process. The balance of the mental, emotional and spiritual aspects of our life is the foundation to understanding the reality of oneness.

When we are in a state of mental and emotional balance; in other words, in heart and mind coherence we will find that it is easier to be an observer and so face life situations from a place of peace, quietness and unconditional love.

The source filled star tetrahedron will help us to balance and integrate the awareness of the Divine Feminine and the Divine Masculine in our lives in a spectacular way.

The deeper spiritual balance of the Divine Feminine (Source Love) and the Divine Masculine (Source Will) will be brought up in episodes of insightfulness in our day to day life; however, this only becomes meaningful from the authenticity of our source self. This can be helped by this source filled structure that is the epitome of balance.

Growth Awareness

The following questions, if answered from a place of integrity, will help you to see where there is a lack of balance in your life.

Think about your days and how much time you spend being present and at peace with yourself. Ask yourself:

Do I fret about things I have to achieve in my day?

Do I allow the pace of my life to affect my health and wellbeing?

Do I react to external emotional happenings in a way that leaves me feeling depleted and uncertain?

Do I feel that another's opinion of me is an important deciding factor in some of my choices?

Do I feel underlying guilt in my choices and decisions?

Do I feel threatened by others at work and/or at home?

If you recognise the feelings and thoughts that these questions evoke as familiar happenings then this source filled shape is a vibrational match to your soul promptings.

All of the above are only small nudges in the direction of your own deeper understanding of what needs to be balanced in your life.

Active Awareness Action

Use the star tetrahedron in a meditation. You may wish to call in the power animals the tiger and the red admiral butterfly.

You may want to keep the previous questions in your mind (or on paper) for a deeper understanding of the imbalances they highlight within you.

Find a quiet place to sit. Take deep cleansing breaths, fill yourself with light. The light will raise your body's vibration.

Feel how present you feel and be aware of your breath as you continue to breathe in a rhythm that is perfect for you.

From this place of being aware of your source self, focus on your heart centre. From that source filled heart space, breathe the shape of the star tetrahedron around you. It is your intention and focus that brings this shape into your awareness.

Now focus on the centre of the source filled star tetrahedron, see it being in line with the centre of the quiet place within your heart centre. Feel the peace and balance that is already within you.

The star tetrahedron that you breathe into creation is the perfect vibrational match for your healing.

The imbalances are already healed and thus balanced. It is just your growing awareness of them that brings them into your consciousness allowing you to understand them. This detachment is part of the healing.

Spend as long as necessary to feel peaceful and have a deeper understanding of the reality of a balanced life and body.

Balance is not something you have to achieve it is something that already is. All you are doing is bringing that reality into your awareness through the help of the universal vibration of love.

ACTIVE AWARENESS
Twelve pointed star

Stellated Dodecahedron

The twelve pointed star is a sacred source filled shape that mirrors the love of the universe, thus it is a geometric shape of completeness.

It can also show us what we need to do to find that completeness within ourselves and it is the perfect vibration to place around ourselves when we are searching for something to make us feel at peace and in a place of contentment and wellbeing.

It is in this space that we find that we are at peace. The peace is found when we stop looking and just become the stillness. This is happiness; from happiness we experience those moments of bliss.

The twelve pointed star can be seen as an accelerator or an amplifier, thus it is the perfect sacred geometric shape to help us to manifest our desires.

If our desire is to be part of the wholeness, the bliss of who we are, we will find that the energetic vibration of this particular shape will help us to understand how to observe our life from a detached point of view.

In other words, the energetic vibration of the twelve pointed star will help us to detach from the physical body, the mental body and all concepts we hold. What is left is the self, the source self; the peace that is Source expressing itself.

Sometimes the need to find our life purpose is part of our growing awareness of our source filled self. This leads us on our quest to find our soul purpose.

Often the catalyst is deep unhappiness or dissatisfaction with our current life. This is actually one of the universal blessings that shows that we are never forgotten. Instead we are being prompted in ways that we cannot ignore.

It is often when we are in a place of uncertainty that we create the need to look at our lives and make changes. However, in the need for guidance we will often look to others for this, spiritual teachers, gurus, yogis, even books and the media. Perhaps we should first consider what our thoughts, feelings and emotions are telling us.

The need for change can be shown through thoughts or feelings. These thoughts, feelings and subsequent emotions are often of a negatively charged nature. Examples of emotions of dis-ease are anger, sadness, suspicion, grief, fearfulness, apprehension, indecisiveness, despair or helplessness leading to depression. In a simplistic way it is any emotion that causes us to feel unhappy that needs to be considered.

Active Awareness

If we are often engulfed by these emotions; consider the fact that we are not in harmony with our soul purpose and it takes these feelings and subsequent emotions to allow us to take stock of our life and redefine who we are and what we want to do to take ourselves back into alignment for the most harmonious outcome of our soul purpose,

What is important to remember is that everything we do in our life is important for our soul expansion and as we acknowledge this it makes it easier to accept that we are on our soul journey. We may be taking the 'hard knock pathway' instead of the pathway that has joy and peace.

These two pathways can be the same, it is just how we define each experience along the path.

Do we see the experience from our ego/personality self that is filled with fear and lack or from our source self that is fearless and filled with love?

This geometric source shape will help us to face our pathway without fear enabling us to see choices and decisions from a place of love filled wisdom.

Active Awareness Action

Surround yourself with this shape through intention using your imagination and purposeful source filled breath.

Meditate for at least thirty minutes surrounded by this shape. Let go of every conceptual part of you and connect with the peace within.

Focus on this question:

What do I need to do to help me experience my soul pathway to its fullest source potential?

Write it down to fully focus on what this means for you.

The energetic vibration of the twelve pointed star will help you to understand what is important for you to focus on at this time. Use this shape to help you manifest your greatest desire.

An advanced way of using this sacred shape is to keep the shape around you for the day and at least once an hour, pause and become aware of the shape around you (using purposeful source breath and imagination).

Feel the excitement of already having in place what you desire, feel the gratitude for this manifestation fill you and walk your day filled with the joy of what you have.

ACTIVE AWARENESS
The Seed Of Life

Consisting of Seven Interlocking Spheres

This sacred source filled shape carries the vibration of the soul journey number seven. It also carries the vibration of the soul journey number one.

The 'seed of life' is Divine Creation and it is part of all life. It is said that it also represents the seven days of creation.

It carries the elements of air, fire, water and earth. It also carries the divinity of love, will and wisdom.

The seed of life represents the seven aspects of unconditional love; compassion, forgiveness, nurturing, passion, loyalty, selflessness and empathy.

This shape is about Source expressing itself through the wonder of planned creation. This can only be done when the desire to create is from the timeless space of unconditional love.

Limitless love or unconditional love has no boundaries and as such it is seen as the seed of all life that can create all possibilities of life.

When we are drawn to this image we are being asked to look at our life through the eyes of being a creator; with the eyes of unconditional love.

Active Awareness

The seed of life's vibrational frequency will always be around you when you intend to manifest something or someone into your life with a passionate desire. It is the unconditional love and deep desire (intent) that resonates with the frequency of the seed of life's vibrational signature.

Do you resonate with the following questions?

Is there something in my life that I feel drawn to change?

Is there something I feel I lack in my life?

The vibrational frequency of this shape will help you to go to the cause of the need to change something in your life. It will help you to see with clarity what you need to heal before you can attract what you want in your life.

It may be that we attract partners that are not kind to us and treat us in a way that we find unacceptable and this could be because on a subconscious level we feel we are not worthy of respect and love; thus, we continue to attract people that treat us in that manner. This leads to a feeling of powerlessness.

We can see it as the hidden part of our psyche; it can be referred to as the forgotten part of the soul, and is sometimes known as the 'shadow self'. These are the hurt emotions and memories that are stored away, the weak and painful side of us hidden from our conscious self; the part of us that once more needs to be seen and recognised. The subsequent healing comes from acknowledgement, compassion and acceptance. This in turn comes from love free from judgement; our unconditional love.

We will also attract this image when we are starting a new phase in our lives. Sometimes an unprecedented happening can occur in our lives that is a catalyst to facilitate a great soul prompting.

At times, the new phase is one we may feel a certain resistance to and as such the frequency of this sacred shape will help us to go to a place of acceptance and surrender.

The vibrational frequency of the seed of life helps our source awareness, which in turn helps us to respond and deal with the change in a way that is far more harmonious for our wellbeing. It is from this peaceful harmony that we will attract the perfect solution to any perceived problem.

This sacred shape can be seen as the perfect germinating vessel for new ideas or new understandings of why a change has come into our lives and how to manifest the perfect outcome that is for our greater happiness.

Active Awareness Action

Use this sacred shape of the seed of life in a meditation. You may wish to call in the power animal the dolphin.

Find a quiet space in nature, ideally somewhere close to water. This will help you to connect to the dolphin. Make sure you are sitting with your feet on the ground.

Take in some deep diaphragm source filled breaths. Do this with the grateful intention that you are connecting to Mother Earth and the Source of Life.

A wonderful way to do this is from your compassionate loving heart. Focus your attention on your heart. Send your love with the intent that it is Source flowing light into the heart of Mother Earth. Imagine her opening her arms to receive this love-light from your heart up to the sun. You are beautifully connected to the Divine Feminine (Mother Earth) and Divine Masculine (Source of Life). Feel them returning their love-light back to you. Now you are ready to create the 'seed of life'.

Using your source breath, breathe the seed of life into your awareness.

It is your passionate desire to understand what you need to do or find out about yourself that makes this a powerful shape.

Further Insights on the Soul Journey Numbers

The following additional information on the soul journey numbers will add extra depth to using soul journey numbers. You may have a favourite number, or a number that you keep noticing over a short period of time.

Number One: Further Insights

The number one can be seen as Divine will, the will of Source.

If you are reading this then it is a reminder to check that you are surrendering to the flow of life around you. This is seen as free will. You are free in your trust of the Divine or Source so that you accept the challenges and blocks and understand that your soul has put this in your pathway to learn or another chance to forgive or heal some karmic event. Letting go and being in the flow of Source is a deep connection to Divine will.

It is time to feel complete, to have an understanding of being complete.

It may also be that it is time to take responsibility for your actions. To do this you need to step into your divine power, this is as simple as acknowledging that you want to take your choices, decisions from the flow of Source, free of judgement. This acknowledgment releases fear and the flow of Source becomes stronger.

The number one also contains the energy of zero or the zero point (the still, quiet place). Nothing (no thing), creates one, and one is in everything. One can be seen as the God atom, the 'Source spark within'. Take time to go to this quiet place, this still point within and feel the clarity and peace that is needed to start a fresh new phase.

The number one is about moving forward and not looking back unless it is with gratitude for the wisdom learnt.

Ask yourself these questions and reflect on your answers:

Do I take responsibility for all aspects of my life?

Do I want a new beginning, but fear change?

Do I live in the past, reliving hurts and anxieties?

Do I fully understand what it is to feel complete?

When you have answered these questions from your heart and reflected on the answers you are understanding the vibration of the soul journey number one and how it can help you to understand that you are one with Source.

One with Source.

Number Two: Further Insights

Two halves make a whole. Two people are in a relationship, or, it can be two opposites that create a harmony of energy. For instance, day and night, the sun and the moon, male and female, black and white.

Therefore the number two makes a powerful vibration, of either harmonising or synchronising opposites.

On our life journey, the number two is very important within a loving relationship. Often people talk about soulmates, the 'one and only'. It seems to be so important that we find the person that makes us truly content and happy, fulfilling all our criteria of what we want in a loving relationship to make us feel whole. To make us as one.

Our relationships are very important to us, but unless we feel complete and whole within ourselves and are able to stand alone (being the perfect one) we cannot expect to make a perfect two.

Therefore, the number two is only complete when it carries the vibration of two whole parts.

Before you enter the vibration of the number two, in these circumstances, it is a good idea to ask yourself:

Am I lonely or just alone?

Am I happy and content, or do I need someone else before I can feel happiness?

As you connect more strongly to Source you become less needy and more independent with the strength of knowing you are never alone. You are part of Source, you are one with Source.

With this knowledge you can decide to start a relationship and it will often be with someone equally connected, who wants a relationship for the joy of it, rather than the need of it. This is when the number two is at its strongest.

However, the vibration of two is found in all relationships. Your relationship with your work and work colleagues, your relationship with your friends, even your relationship with a challenging situation.

Once you realise the importance of being complete and aware of our source connection on a daily basis, the relationships on your life journey become source filled.

Sometimes in relationships your soul directs you to where you may find huge challenges for soul growth but if you start with the energy of one and be aware of how connected you are, it helps the vibration of two and your completeness will positively affect any relationship in your life.

Two is a sacred vibration of spiritual balance.

Number Three: Further Insights

The number three carries the vibration of both one and two.

We now know the importance of feeling complete, and taking this feeling into our relationships whether these are with other people, with our career, our family or a personal situation.

We also need to consider the sacred geometry of the number three.

This is the higher consciousness aspect of the number one, which is helping the personality self to become Source Conscious. This allows us to acknowledge the fact that we are indeed filled with Source Consciousness.

The acceptance of this allows us to fully embrace our own source selves, which in turn helps us to see all our relationships, and indeed ourselves, from a higher perspective.

Seeing ourselves, and what we have done, in this way which is free of judgement, allows us to forgive ourselves and move forward.

We then find that within our relationships we no longer react with hurt, pain or aspects of fear, but instead we respond from a place of love.

We need to take responsibility for our actions and behaviour, both in all our relationships and also in how we see ourselves. We are then working in a Trinity with our Divine Mother and our Divine Father.

It is time now to be conscious of the source vibration of the number three.

Look at all your relationships. Study them from your source self.

What can you change?

From the perspective of your Source Conscious self:

Look at yourself. How do you see yourself?

It is helpful to make a list and learn from your past relationships. This will help you to understand and let go of past fears. You can then start from a fearless place, the place that is in all of us.

That fearless place is our source self.

Number Four: Further Insights

The number four is sacred; it enables us to bring a sense of groundedness and stability into our various relationships. Surrounded by the energy of the number four, we can also understand the broader aspect of the number three - the understanding of how we walk every day in Divine love on the pathway of Divine will through the understanding of Divine wisdom. The number four helps us feel safe and secure while on this Source Conscious pathway.

The number four carries the vibration of 'hope' from the present moment, allowing us to anticipate our dreams and thus enabling their creation and realisation. Remember, a good way to be present is to ground oneself. To ground ourselves, we can call on Mother Earth to help us, bringing structure and stability to our lives and the potential to be fully conscious of our Source self. This is when we can welcome the gift of hope.

The energy of the number four is present in the vibration of Mother Earth, and her expression of love is what we call nature. Every tree, flower, and rock carries this energy because Mother Earth overflows with the vibration of four. When we immerse ourselves in nature, Mother Earth's expression of love, whether walking in a forest or swimming in the sea, fills our senses with her love. At these times, we can heal, feeling as if the hand of nature is leading us to become aware of what we need to do to increase our well being. It can be an idea, a knowing, or a moment of clarity where we can improve our lifestyle.

This takes 'hope' to the next step - trust. Trust comes from knowing that we are in the arms of Mother Earth, or we can say, the arms of Source. As material beings holding the light of Source, we often trust what is real and beautiful, which is why we identify with nature. Perhaps we identify with a sturdy oak or the soft flow of a stream. It is this identification that helps us trust the insights that a connection with nature gives us. These insights are inspired by nature, but it is the loving song/sounds of Mother Earth carrying the energy of four that helps us awaken to our Source Consciousness.

The spiritually stabilising number four enables us to awaken to our Source Consciousness.

The number four is a key to our awakening Source Consciousness.

Number Five: Further Insights

The number five vibrates with the energy of Gaia. It holds the creativity of our human form.

If we think about our own bodies, our own human temples, we will notice that we have hands with five fingers, and feet with five toes. We also have a head, two arms and two legs, which also makes five.

We are the living embodiment of five.

The number five is about the choices and decisions that we take in our material world. It is also the first step of the three stages over the bridge between the material world and the spiritual world (numbers seven and nine are the further two numbers representing these stages).

As this is the first step, when we are experiencing the vibration of the number five in our lives, our challenges are often very materially based: our finances, our housing, our physical health etc.

This can lead to a feeling of being trapped. Therefore, the number five leads to an understanding of true freedom.

This is the first stage of awakening and we begin to understand that freedom can be an illusion until we see that true freedom is the understanding that we are Source.

The number five can also result in our feeling restless and constantly seeking something. This is our higher source self guiding us to find our correct soul pathway through the vibration of the number five.

The vibration of five will come into our lives when we are stagnated with blocks and fear; it will often help us to make huge changes and different choices. The number five carries the energy of courage and determination.

However, if we have not taken that first step over the bridge, then the number five can cause us to feel overwhelmed with the illusion of fear. This is a time when people will seek spiritual help.

The number five is at its highest vibration when we are aware of awakening and allowing balance and constant flow into our lives.

The number five can be seen as the lesson plan for our life here on Earth.

Number Six: Further Insights

The number six carries the vibration of the number three in a more awakened state where we are meant to take more responsibility for our soul journey.

Whilst the number three carries the joy of discovery and the sweet nectar of knowledge, being a part of Source and 'all that is', the number six is telling us to use this knowledge now for the greater good of our soul companions, or in other words, for our Earth family.

This brings with it greater enlightenment and the wisdom that grows as we use this sacred vibration.

The number six is always about learning more, being at times the teacher and at times the student, making a stand for what we know is right and walking the path of integrity.

The number six is also about taking responsibility for the choices we make and being able to see soul growth in our challenges.

Taking responsibility may also be a time when we need to take charge, lead or be in control of a situation whether it be at work, socially or at home. Often this happens when we are least prepared or new at a particular challenge. This soul growth step is about how we deal with the challenges and choices we take.

It is an opportunity to take decisions from the intuitive heart and not solely the mind, whilst embracing the wisdom of others. We allow the grace of Source to flow through us.

This releases all the limitations that our fears place around us. We are at last tasting freedom.

In challenging times use your intention to walk in the vibration of the number six and this will enable you to gather Source Consciousness around you and to become aware of seeing and acting with greater clarity.

The sacred vibration of the number six may help you to serve others, as you have always intended, at a soul level.

The number six will bring us true freedom as we progress on our soul journey.

Number Seven: Further Insights

The number seven is connected to source breath (gently breathing in and out through the nose using the diaphragm to inhale and gently relaxing the diaphragm to gently and automatically breathe out). When we are surrounded by the vibration of the number seven, we are conscious of a strong awareness of breathing in Source. Breath is no longer just an automatic action, it is felt as the breath of Source.

The number seven carries the strong vibration of Source.

The number seven is also found in different formats and combinations within our lives, for example, there are seven days in a week, seven days of creation, seven colours of the rainbow.

The number seven is also the combination of the Source Consciousness of the number three and the stability of the number four. In this way it connects our personality self and spiritual self at a higher level.

Remember that the numbers five, seven and nine are three steps to bridging our earthly lives and the light being that we are. The number seven is a midway point of spiritual awakening, and we become more aware of the process of evolving towards the light.

When people are surrounded by the energy of the number seven they often find themselves being pulled towards teaching or healing others. The spiritual pull is great and the need to remain spiritually balanced becomes greater, the awareness of our energy centres grows stronger, and we also become more sensitive to the lack of positivity (fear) in others.

This can then bring about a feeling for the need for protection. There are many types of spiritual protection. The sphere of light carries the vibration of seven, nine and eleven as well as the vibrations of the source filled rainbow colours, so this is a very powerful sacred shape to have around us. We can surround ourselves and our energy centres with a sphere of pure Divine light to protect us on all levels.

The number seven is unique as it offers the spiritual protection we sometimes need for our own personality self, as it helps us to detach and to be aware of illusory fears.

The number seven is a highly vibrational number and it is often found in the vibration of synchronistic events! This is when we really are in sync with our Divine will.

The number seven strengthens our connection to Source.

Number Eight: Further Insights

The soul journey number eight is about creating and manifesting.

The number four is about grounding and stability, and the number eight is about building our life on those strong foundations.

The number eight is also about eternity, so whatever we create or manifest is for ever, at an energetic level.

When our creations are positive they are a window to our soul; however, when we create through fear it can be seen as another opportunity to re-address our soul lesson.

Create with joy in mind so that the connection to Source is strong.

The number eight is about manifesting and abundance once our spiritual and physical foundations have been put in place.

Eight is also about creating a flow in our lives, which in turn allows the rebirth of our source creating abilities to become our reality.

Look at your life, and ask yourself these questions:

What foundations have I put in place to call in what I need?

Am I spiritually grounded every day?

Am I creating a flow in my life by clearing spiritual blocks, karma etc?

Am I creating a flow in my life by clearing physical clutter?

Am I creating a constant flow in my life by acknowledging the connection to Source with gratitude and humility?

When we are drawn to the number eight it is often when we need to expand, we need to go further with a project or a creative idea. This could involve moving house or changing jobs. It could even be that we want to explore new avenues or ideas socially, at work, or in our general life. Although this is exciting, any fear surrounding our decisions, could attract difficulties. This is when surrounding yourself with the energy of the tiger or master Moses will help to face the adventure with the anticipation of success, this in turn draws success towards us.

The number eight will help our lives to flow and help us to manifest.

Number Nine: Further Insights

The energy of the number nine carries the vibration of 3 + 3 + 3 or 333.

This is like the Trinity at a deeper level of understanding.

The number nine completes the connection of the bridge of living life from our ego self to consciously living life from our source self. This bridge carries the energy of five, seven and nine.

To recap: five is the energy that we draw towards us on our linear life here on Earth, the challenges and blocks that arise when we are swamped in the materialistic aspects.

The energy of seven gives us the tools that can help us to heal and find the strength to see our lives from a different perspective which in turn helps the awakening of our conscious awareness.

When we start drawing the energy of nine towards us it is when we are ready to surrender to the flow, the will of Divine within, to open our hearts to the love of the Divine within and to see our life here with the knowing of the Divine wisdom.

We no longer feel separate. We realise that we are one with 'all that is'.

When we have the number nine vibration around us, we find that we are more easily able to see challenges from our source self and detach more freely from any fears.

Within this vibration we notice that our service is on a greater scale. We often find ourselves in positions of authority and have the responsibility of helping many other souls.

This can also have its challenges, as sometimes it is a burden of love. Our challenges come from a place of deeper soul work. They will not be as obvious and will be more spiritual in nature.

When the vibration of the number nine surrounds us, we find that the wisdom of our soul is more easily accessible. We have a deeper understanding of why we have had certain challenges in our lives.

The vibration of the number nine is often found when we are living in the present moment. It has the feeling of balance and we find that we are able to see what is needed to bring greater spiritual balance to our lives.

When we see the power of the number nine as combinations of the number three then we find that our day is flooded with Source Consciousness.

We become aware of our own Source Consciousness.

Number Eleven: Further Insights

The number eleven carries the vibration of a double one and encourages a deep knowing connection to the soul in this lifetime.

This is echoed by the fact that the number eleven also carries the vibration of the number two and the number nine. This means that the number eleven carries the wisdom and Source Consciousness of the number nine and the deep commitment of the number two.

This is shown in the relationship between the enlightened personality self and the soul journey that has been put in place. This happens as the separation between the personality self and the source self gradually becomes less.

This in turn makes the relationship between the source self and Source have a greater effect on the life journey, showing itself as the driving need to serve Source and be in service to others.

As already mentioned the number eleven carries the strong vibration of the number two and is also a double one. This strongly emphasises the wholeness in all spiritual relationships.

This can be seen in the relationship between the ego personality and source self and the growing awareness that in fact there is no separateness, only one, and that one is Source.

The number eleven carries the vibration of 'all that is'; that we are all equal and at the same time 'no thing', we just are.

The number eleven carries the invisible vibration of the number ten. This is the acknowledgment of one and the zero point. It states again the end of a phase and the beginning of another, this cycle is never ending or eternity.

Therefore, the number eleven indicates that we are Source Infinity.

POWER ANIMAL: BLUE WHALE

The blue whale carries the vibration of the soul
journey number one

*If your birthdate adds up to the soul journey number one (so
your soul contract number is one) or you draw the vibration of the
number one towards you then you will be helped and guided by
this power animal.*

The qualities and traits that the blue whale will help
us with are:

completeness   stability   profoundness
the concept of timelessness
reaching higher dimensions   righteousness   honourable intentions
worthiness   integrity

These are the qualities of Source within

However, on our journey of source evolvement and as part of our soul experience
we may relate to, or draw towards us, these challenging traits and situations, or subtle
echoes of them:

boorishness   anger issues   jealousy   ill health   indiscretion   impatience
anxiety   feelings of inadequacy and loss   lack of judgement

These are the gifts of grace from Source

This magnificent power animal will always be with us when we are planning a new
adventure or entering a new phase on our soul journey.

*If you resonate with the blue whale's energy, or your birthdate adds up to the soul journey
number one, you will find that you will be involved in helping others.*

This will be in a profound manner and your integrity and honour will be a banner of your worth.

*This can be in all walks of life but always in service to those who are drawn to your energy. The
light of the blue whale will help you to see the merit and value in others.*

The reality of being one with 'all that is' will be magnified when we draw the energy
of the blue whale towards us; this is a feeling of completeness.

However, we can be side tracked by our own and others fearful perceptions of what
is right for us, and this can influence our decisions and take us away from the feeling of
completeness.

The blue whale surrounding us with its understanding of oneness of all that is can
help us back into a peaceful alignment with our source self.

We learn to trust our higher judgment and Source.

Also, being surrounded in the ancient wisdom of this power animal will help us to
find the light of our soul pathway. Equally, it is the act of surrendering to 'Divine Love'
that is the key to connecting to the higher dimensions within our source self.

When we are called into spiritual service and also drawn to the vibration of the soul journey number one, it will often lead us to the higher dimensions of source wisdom.

Our quest for timeless source wisdom will be supported by the blue whale, who in itself is timeless and can help us to understand that all exists in the moment.

When we are surrounded by the light of this power animal everything becomes possible.

We are shown at these times the many possibilities in our future reality, through universal signs and insights from our source self. It is up to us to find the strength of purpose (Divine Will) to go forward on an enlightened evolving pathway.

Every sentient being will, at some time, be touched by the vibration of the number one in this profound way, it is how we interpret this energy that defines us.

As we will have seen, every number carries the pattern of the number one. This means that we all carry the limitless possibilities of Source.

Those of us who resonate with the vibration of the soul journey number one and the power animal that is the blue whale, will often be called to lead others to this greater awareness.

This can be done through practical teaching and guidance or purely as a beacon of integrity and honour.

When we identify with the size and might of the blue whale and the completeness of all that is, we will bring stability into every new phase or event.

We can, if we choose, surrender to the timeless strength and magnitude of the blue whale and experience these qualities within our reality.

POWER ANIMAL: GOLDEN EAGLE and GOLDFINCH

The golden eagle and the goldfinch carry the vibration of soul journey number two

If your birthdate adds up to the soul journey number two or you draw the vibration of the number two towards you, you will be guided and helped by these power animals.

The qualities and traits that the golden eagle will help us with are:

mastery   fame   radiance   abundance   spiritual writings
spiritual counselling for families

The qualities or traits that the goldfinch will help us with are:

supportiveness   protectiveness   benevolence
open mindedness   spiritual channelling

These are the qualities of Source within

However, on our journey of source evolvement and as part of our soul experience we may relate to, or draw towards us these challenging traits or situations, or subtle echoes of them:

animosity towards others   belligerence   prejudice   intolerance
gloominess   neediness   defeatism   faithlessness   mistrust

These are the gifts of grace from Source

The golden eagle's light will surround us when we are dealing with any sort of relationship with others, especially if we are growing in our mastery of spiritual enlightenment.

We are all potential masters; however, when we are drawing the soul journey vibration of the number two towards us we are often dealing with the most challenging lesson in life and that is the relationship between our personality self and our higher self.

This is often a life journey of growing spiritual awareness and part of this will be helping others. This includes all types of counselling, family therapy, therapeutic or spiritual writing or facilitating. Whatever we are drawn to will be part of our growing mastery.

The golden eagle will spread its protective wings around us if we are out of our comfort zone, especially when our soul journey takes us to where we are in contact with a huge number of people. This is becoming more common with the growth of the media and internet interaction.

If this resonates with you, take time with the golden eagle and make sure that you are being led by your source self for the greater good of many.

When we draw this magnificent power animal towards us, we will resonate with its huge radiance. This is because we are mirroring the radiance of Source and are in alignment with our source self.

This is a gift that we can take to others in our lives, affecting them in a positive uplifting way. We become the light of Source radiating outwards and our conduct is a beacon to those with whom we come into contact.

The golden eagle represents abundance and when we draw the light of this power animal towards us we will find previously unnoticed abundance in our lives. The appreciation of abundance in its many forms becomes clearer to us, especially in our relationships.

The goldfinch will help us to connect to our spiritual guides and channelling will be as natural as breathing. We can all connect to the beings of light if we choose to; however, it is when channelling is part of our core purpose that we will often be drawn to the goldfinch.

If this is part of your soul journey the goldfinch and the vibration of the number two will resonate strongly with you at these times.

Part of the growing awareness of our source self is the ability to be open minded and receptive to ideas and knowledge that we encounter. It is our strong connection to our source self that protects us from falsehoods and others' limited perceptions.

If we are surrounded by the energy of the goldfinch we will be guided and supported at these times.

Being drawn to the vibration of the soul journey number two and the benevolence of the goldfinch helps us to trust our instincts and insights when dealing with others.

POWER ANIMAL: THREE DOVES

The dove carries the vibration of the soul journey number three. However they can also be seen as the three separate doves:

The dove of peace
The dove of fulfilment
The dove of universal truth

If your birthdate adds up to the soul journey number three or you draw the vibration of the number three towards you then you will be helped and guided by the three doves

The qualities and traits that the dove will help us with are:

peacefulness   fulfilment   universal truth
hope   dedication   gratitude

These are the qualities of Source within

The white dove is a messenger from the higher dimensions.

However, on our journey of source evolvement and as part of our soul experience we may relate to, or draw towards us, these challenging traits and situations, or subtle echoes of them:

conflict within   deep restlessness   dissatisfaction   despair
faithlessness   being uncommitted   apathy   scepticism

These are the gifts of grace from Source

These three doves help us to find the deep peace within. Peacefulness can be seen as being present and in alignment with our source self. Peace is found when we are at one with all aspects of ourselves. There is no inner conflict, just a sense of quietness. It is from this stillness that is our sacred self, that we can see our blessings, enabling us to express our gratitude for not only the joyful experiences but also our challenging soul growth lessons.

It is the dove of peace that will surround us with its source light and help us to find that inner quietness. It is from here that we can see our hopes and desires from the perspective of our higher self.

When our hopes and desires are seen from our present self we are able to match our frequency to what we hope for. This is manifesting.

We, as beings of light, strive for universal truth. There are so many conflicting ideas and opinions that it can be confusing, especially when we are on our spiritual journey.

We can be creatures of habit as we spend a lot of our time in the past, also working on automatic pilot with thoughts and programs that are part of our subconscious.

This means that when we are seeking the truth we need to be in a mindful state and open to the universal promptings of what is right for us at this moment. In this way we will find that we become in tune with our source self and so will find that we are able to discern the universal truth that is part of us. It can be that we gain this wisdom from other spiritual gurus or spiritual writings.

If we are drawn to these three power doves we are often looking for our core purpose. This brings us the feeling of fulfilment which, in turn, leads us to inner peace.

Spending time in meditation with the dove of fulfilment will help us to further understand our core purpose. It is this understanding and enlightenment that will help us to dedicate our being to our soul journey.

It is important to recognise that feelings of restlessness, inner conflict and dissatisfaction are often promptings from our higher selves to show us that we are not in alignment with our core or soul purpose. We will find that often the promptings become huge life changes in order for us to change direction. Despite this, we will have learnt soul lessons that will benefit us and others on our future life journey.

When we work simultaneously with this power animal and the vibration of three we are able to communicate strongly with our source self. This will draw the messages of light towards us.

Messages of light are brought in many ways, such as synchronistic events, repetition of number sequences, a deep knowing, white feathers and many more. Remember all messages will be understood when taking the time to be present in our source self.

Become the dove of universal truth and breathe the truth of the message into your consciousness.

POWER ANIMAL: DEER (STAG and DOE)

The deer (stag and doe) carries the vibration of soul journey number four.

If your birthdate adds up to the soul journey number four or you draw the vibration of the number four towards you, then you will be helped and guided by this power animal.

The qualities and traits that the stag will help us with are:

solidness   composure   resilience   purity   steadfastness

The qualities and traits that the doe will help us with are:

gentleness   compassion   spiritual insights
sentimentality   empathy   mindfulness

These are the qualities of Source within

However, on our journey of source evolvement and as part of our soul experience we may relate to, or draw towards us, these challenging traits and situations, or subtle echoes of them:

vengefulness   implacability   sternness   imperviousness
living in the past   mindless eating   apprehension   suspicion
melodrama   inflexibility

These are the gifts of grace from Source

The stag will help us to stay grounded and in a state of composure and patience when we are being tested, or in a place of conflict with another.

Often when the vibration of the number four is around us we will be helping others to achieve this equanimity and calmness as well. This will be in a teaching or supportive role.

These roles may also need the resilience of one who does not give in to unjust situations but remains true to their convictions, at the same time remaining flexible and open minded to other's insightful suggestions.

The stag will help with the leadership qualities of constancy and steadfastness, this will induce loyalty and trust in others.

Whenever our life journey takes us towards leadership, headship or positions of power, the energy of the stag and doe will help us to remain constantly in the present, being mindful of our source selves and enabling us to lead in an empowered authentic manner.

The stag's energy helps us to see honour in others, to do this we will need to be in the purest state of vibration that we can manage. This can be a life changing decision. We may need to look at every aspect of our lives that could affect our vibration.

The vibration of the number four will help us with purifying our food intake. The energy of the stag helps us to be aware of our body's needs. This means that we are getting the support of this power animal in helping us to discern between habit forming comfort food and high vibrational energy food.

'You are what you eat'! This concept may be of huge importance to us; however, tackling this reality and helping others to do the same is when we will draw this power animal towards us.

The energy of the doe will be drawn around us when we are on the spiritual path of service to others, especially when caring for others in a way that needs compassion.

Compassion is a strong quality found in those of us that have the birth number four; however, we first need to have the unconditional love for ourselves and this can be a huge part of our soul mission.

Being compassionate towards others is a projection of our source self and it is the recognition of love in others that draws the compassion and limitless love from us.

It is this heartfelt compassion that enables us to empathise with others.

We draw the energy of the doe towards us when we are being mindful and in the present and this is often when we have the most soul enriching insights. It is these spiritual insights that will effectively help us on our soul journey.

This will enhance our service to others in many different ways. The soft gentle ways of the doe will help us to be one with all nature and the Earth itself.

If our soul journey leads us to resonate strongly with nature and Mother Earth, this will often lead us to work with crystals, trees, flowers and animals.

POWER ANIMAL: JAGUAR

The jaguar carries the vibration of the soul journey number five.

If your birthdate adds up to the soul journey number five, or you draw the vibration of the number five towards you then you will be helped and guided by this power animal.

The qualities and traits that the jaguar will help us with are:

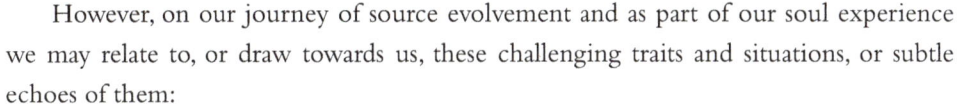

power   resilience   emotional balance   faithfulness
attraction   loyalty

These are the qualities of Source within

However, on our journey of source evolvement and as part of our soul experience we may relate to, or draw towards us, these challenging traits and situations, or subtle echoes of them:

resistance   emotional upheaval   powerlessness   inadequacy
untrustworthiness   weakness   giving up easily

These are the gifts of grace from Source

Part of our spiritual awakening is claiming back the power we have given away in this lifetime (and others). The jaguar will help us to empower ourselves.

In times when we are leading or guiding it is important to differentiate between controlling from our ego fear self and guiding from our higher selves.

Many times, on our life journey, we will face challenges that need us to be resilient. This is not easy if we feel overwhelmed and fearful. The jaguar helps us to face our challenges, especially the challenges that seem to have no end to the pain and dis-ease.

The jaguar helps us to find the blessings within our challenge; appreciation is the fuel that we need to remain resilient.

Our life as humans can lead to huge emotional disharmony which in turn can create a reality that is fear based and the opposite to what we want or need.

The jaguar will help us to have more clarity through the 'heart knowing' of what is best for ourselves.

This calm and balanced power animal will help us to navigate through the sea of dis-eased emotions and recognise what thoughts and thought patterns are causing this.

This is often called shadow work, which is becoming aware of what is hidden in the subconscious. When we feel a resistance to this, the power animal helps us to understand the fear based issue, or memory behind this.

The jaguar will help us to recognise the difference between faith and belief. We need to have faith and trust that we are Source and from this trust we can be open to many belief systems. However, as our conscious awareness grows, certain beliefs and belief structures may not be in alignment with our enlightenment.

Certain belief systems may be limiting and this is when trusting or having faith in our source self is crucial.

It is the understanding that we are all one that will help us to be open minded and loyal to our true self, our source self.

We are part of the law of attraction, which is how we manifest; however, due to our fears, we may manifest what we do not want due to our subconscious desires. This is part of our life journey. We discover the parts of our subconscious mind that are attracting and manifesting future happenings that cause us disharmony.

However, if we acknowledge that we are powerful, resilient and trusting creators we can be honest with ourselves and be in the truth of what we want and do not want.

The jaguar helps us to be loyal to our own truth. This may mean we need to find the strength within to face others, especially when we face others' disbelief or incredulity. It is at these times that we draw the vibration of five and the light of the jaguar around us.

Connecting with this power animal will help us on our soul growth pathway. We are source beings in a material body and accepting the help of the jaguar helps us to become more aware of this universal truth.

POWER ANIMAL: SWAN (COB and PEN)

The swan (cob and pen) carry the vibration of soul
journey number six.

*If your birthdate adds up to the soul journey number six or
you draw the vibration of the number six towards you then you
will be helped and guided by this power animal.*

The qualities and traits that the swan will help
us with are:

consideration   decisiveness   kindness
speaking your truth
unconditional love   acceptance of miracles
appreciation of beauty and grace in life

These are the qualities of Source within

However, on our journey of source evolvement and as part of our soul experience
we may relate to, or draw towards us, these challenging traits and situations, or subtle
echoes of them:

fear of speaking your truth   distrust in synchronicity
judgemental unkindness   self hate   egocentricity   selfishness

These are gifts of grace from Source

Consideration for others can only be achieved once we have consideration towards
our own needs and desires. If we choose to deny ourselves, it would be impossible to see
others' needs from a place of empathy and objectivity.

To be firm and decisive is a part of spiritual discipline when it is applied from our
source selves. The trait of firmness has to be free of our personality self in order to be
full of kindness, compassion and understanding and yet be able to guide the situation or
person in the highest possible way.

To achieve this, we need to deal with ourselves in a similar manner.

The grace and beauty of the swan will be qualities that will be reflected in us when
we are immersed in the energy of this power animal. If this is our soul contract power
animal, it is about acknowledging the beauty and grace in ourselves which then allows us
to see beauty in others.

To find beauty in life, even in places where there is hardship or disharmony, is an act
of appreciation; it is the appreciation of what we have and what our life journey shows us
that is the catalyst for this to occur.

Often it is in dire situations that we see other's acts of random kindness and love
allowing us to see the beauty within.

To see beauty in others or a situation is to mirror the beauty in ourselves.

An act of kindness that is purely from love, is a gift that we choose to give or receive. This act of love requires no compensation.

We will find that the swan (pen) helps us to see acts of kindness from our source self, enabling us to accept. It is the ego personality that will often struggle to accept acts of kindness.

To be kind is to be fully connected to our source self, enabling us to see we are actually being kind to ourselves.

The power animal the swan (cob) will help us to accept many synchronistic happenings as gentle reminders from Source to open our eyes to life around us. Often, we are in habitual routines and we are not always mindful and need these promptings to bring us to the present to make a source filled choice or decision.

What we may think of as a miracle is in fact often the perfect source alignment with a soul commitment.

Miracles are seen as a happening not explained by scientific or natural law. It is easier to see these miracles as Divine Timing.

It is with the help of the source energy of the swan that we can recognise this.

If we have drawn this power animal towards us then we are meant to speak from our authenticity. This will be the source attribute that is the strongest when dealing with others. Our core soul purpose will be found more easily when we look at all aspects of ourselves.

We must question our thoughts, our choices and decisions. We need to decide whether our thoughts reflect our true selves or, perhaps, our fearful subconscious patterns and habits.

The swan will be with us constantly when we question ourselves with the intention of being authentic and speaking from our hearts.

POWER ANIMAL: DOLPHIN

The dolphin carries the vibration of the soul journey number seven

If your birthdate adds up to the soul journey number seven or you draw the vibration of the number seven towards you then you will be helped and guided by this power animal.

The qualities and traits that the dolphin resonates with and will help us with are:

playfulness   expressions of joy   spiritual wisdom
living life to the full   enlightenment   perceptiveness
helping others on their soul journey
energetic healing   mastering your 'rhythm of breath'
strong connection to animals   deep love for Mother Earth

These are the qualities of Source within

However, on our journey of source evolvement and as part of our soul experience we may relate to, or draw towards us, these challenging traits and situations, or subtle echoes of them:

lack of self worth   no vitality   depression   melancholy   misery
shyness   irrational behaviour   recklessness
lack of consideration   self absorption   feeling lost

These are the gifts of grace from Source

The dolphin will show us how to express the joyful inner child in us. We, as adults, often forget how to be playful, how to express our joy from our hearts without the bindings and limitations of others' expectations.

The ability to spread joy and happiness around us is especially present when we are resonating with the vibration of the soul journey number seven. This will also draw the joyous energy of the dolphin towards us.

It is these qualities that enable us to 'live life to the full'.

This means looking at our life and not feeling cheated or having regrets. It is when we gain a lot from life by trying new experiences, keeping busy, always with a deep feeling of contentment.

It is important to look at your own life. What brings you joy and contentment?

It is the dolphin that will help us to achieve our 'bucket list' of desires.

The dolphin will help us on our spiritual journey towards enlightenment. This means we may be pulled towards the knowledgeable teachings of others in our quest for spiritual growth.

However, if the teacher's spiritual wisdom does not resonate, it will often be a sign to trust our higher intuition and our source self to guide us to other enlightened teachers.

We can connect to the wisdom of certain ascended masters; these masters will always help and guide us (pages 158 to 161).

The dolphin will also help us to connect to our spirit guides and any other resonating power animals.

It is important to remember to be constantly present and in a state of mindfulness in the search for spiritual wisdom.

It is the vibration of the soul journey number seven that helps us to understand the importance of our breath and it is the dolphin that can help us to find the perfect 'rhythm of breath' that is uniquely ours.

If being a spiritual teacher is part of your soul journey, the dolphin will help you to connect to your higher self for the purpose of finding the best way for you to be in spiritual service to others.

If we are drawn to energy healing, it is this power animal that will help us towards the clarity and perception needed to resonate clearly with the correct healing modality.

However, it is often our perceived limitations that will prevent us from going forward. This is when the dolphin can help us to acknowledge our fears and anxieties in order to detach from them.

Healing can be directed towards any part of our material and spiritual existence. Healing the planet Earth and helping others to appreciate her beauty and many gifts will always draw the energy of the dolphin towards us.

When we call on the dolphin, we will always feel that the energy of this incredibly wise and joyful power animal is with us. This is especially strong when we are immersed in water.

We may even have a desire to swim with the dolphins. It is with the help of the vibration of the soul journey number seven and surrounding ourselves with the energy of the dolphin that will help us to manifest this desire.

POWER ANIMALS: TIGER and RED ADMIRAL BUTTERFLY

The tiger and the red admiral butterfly both carry
the vibration of the soul journey number eight

*If your birthdate adds up to the soul journey number eight or
you draw the vibration of the number eight towards you then you
will be helped and guided by these power animals.*

The qualities and traits that the tiger will help us with are:

purpose   fortitude   stamina

spiritual awareness   discernment

inspiring others   determination   competency

spiritual leadership   authenticity   mediation

The qualities and traits that the red admiral butterfly will help us with are:

transmutation   meditating

preparation for change   being present

These are the qualities of Source within

However, on our journey of source evolvement and as part of our soul experience we may relate to, or draw towards us, these challenging traits and situations, or subtle echoes of them:

mental illness   confusion   dis-ease   stagnancy   fear of change

bitterness   inconsistency   indecision   egocentricity   easily threatened

These are gifts of grace from Source

The tiger is a formidable and purposeful power animal and when we are surrounded in this powerful energy it will feel that anything can be achieved.

The stamina and ability to 'never give up' are the qualities that we are helped with when we are surrounded in the vibration of the soul journey number eight and the energy of the invincible tiger.

The tiger will help us when our intention is to help and guide others on a spiritual journey. When this is part of Divine Will, the spiritual discipline and fortitude can bring about challenges.

The challenges may come in the form of opposition to the teachings and wisdom we are sharing so 'being in the present' with our source self is vital in order to separate ego from true authenticity in ourselves and others.

If you find that your soul pathway leads you to this place of antagonism and resistance, imagine walking with this power animal at your side and face these challenges with discernment and the truth of who you are.

True authenticity can only happen when we are in our source self in the present moment.

The art of meditation is an effective way of helping us to remain in the present moment. This takes dedication and practice.

If we choose, we can make our day a meditational practice by intending to keep ourselves focused on the present moment. In other words, being mindful of every small act and being fully aware of when our thoughts are on past actions or worry about future happenings.

This mindful power animal can be with us throughout our day helping us to stay immersed in our 'source presence'.

The insightful power animal, the red admiral butterfly, will also surround us with its source light when we are meditating and help us to further understand our source self.

It is in this deep introspective state that we may find areas of energy in our auric field that need transmuting. This power animal will help us to understand this energy and transmute it to source light.

When a phase in our life journey ends and the emotions we feel are grief and despair, we will always draw the soul journey vibration of the number eight and these two power animals to us.

They help us to accept and move forward.

At times our soul journey will take us towards unwanted change. This may create feelings of disharmony, inconsistency and indecision. This is caused by fearful thought patterns from our subconscious mind. Fear creates the illusion of duality and we will feel isolated and separated from our source self.

It is the vibration of the soul journey number eight and these power animals that will help us to step away from thoughts of fear and anxiety, enabling us to look in a positive way at the change in our life.

This action can only be achieved when we are present in our awakened conscious self. We become consciously at one with our source self and in turn at one with these power animals and their supportive energetic signature.

POWER ANIMAL: WHITE HUSKY

The white husky carries the vibration of the soul journey number nine

If your birthdate adds up to the soul journey number nine or you draw the vibration of number nine towards you then you will be helped and guided by this power animal.

The qualities and traits the white husky will help us with are:

endurance   heart and mind coherence
perseverance   spiritual discipline
connection to Higher Beings of Light
training as an apprentice spiritual master
seeing life from an objective point of view

These are the qualities of Source within

However, on our journey of source evolvement and as part of our soul experience we may relate to, or draw towards us, these challenging traits and situations, or subtle echoes of them:

disillusionment   feelings of unexplained loss   sadness and deprivation
never seeking answers within, only outside oneself   unworthiness
drawing repetitive challenges into your reality   overindulgence

These are gifts of grace from Source

The blue eyed white husky is a vibration of the purest energy and we are helped with acts of purifying and cleansing when we are surrounded by the energy of this power animal.

This may call for acts of endurance and courage as huge changes are undertaken. This can be moving house, changing partners, lifestyle changes even belief systems. These situations are best undertaken when we are in a state of heart and mind coherence.

This is when we are balanced and in alignment with our source self. When we are grounded and connected we are aware of our source self, but fully committed to our earthly school of learning. This brings us happiness and acceptance of who we are and it is then that we can see our 'core purpose'.

The white husky helps us to take responsibility for our actions. Often this is not easy as, from our three dimensional perspective, we tend to see that 'the other is to blame' or we feel the situation that is causing us distress is beyond our control.

It is the pureness of the white husky's vibration that will help us to be spiritually disciplined in actions that encourage us to step back from blame and rather towards seeing that we can take control of how we respond to our own life situations.

Ask yourself this: Do I experience my life from my fearful emotions and feelings?

How does this make me feel?

See your life from another perspective; from the part of yourself that can be objective about its findings, free from judgement and filled the love.

You will find that you no longer draw a repetitive challenge towards you, rather you create what you need to experience from your source self.

When we intend to go into the Source within, to understand why we react instead of responding from love and responsibility, we are then facing the master within our self.

We are seeing our true self.

The vibration of the soul journey number nine and the light of the white husky will be drawn towards us when we accept that we are an 'apprentice master'. **Spiritual growth takes spiritual discipline.** This can be seen as the alchemy of the Divine Love, Will and Wisdom that is within us all.

It is this dedication that leads us to our core purpose. This can be a life commitment and often brings us into the service of helping others to find their own life purpose.

We are not alone but it is our choice to ask for help and guidance from the higher beings of light.

It is a joy and a great comfort to realise that we are being supported and helped by ascended masters, angelic beings, power animals and other high vibrational beings of light. When we draw the vibration of the soul journey number nine and the traits of endurance and perseverance of the white husky towards us we become more aware of the presence of these wise and loving beings.

POWER ANIMAL: THE HARE

The hare expresses infinite possibilities. It helps us to move beyond our limitations. It shows a different perspective.

It then helps us to find the internal strength to face the limitations that are self inflicted. The hare will also help us to understand the limitations others place on us enabling us to move away from them or deal with the situation in a different way in order to break through their resistance.

The hare helps us to see the synchronicity in many happenings, showing us that life is living through us, we just need to acknowledge it and say thank you.

POWER ANIMAL: SNOW LEOPARD

The snow leopard carries the vibration of the soul journey number eleven

If your birth date adds up to the soul journey number eleven or you draw the vibration of the number eleven towards you then you will be helped and guided by this power animal.

The snow leopard is intrinsically a shape changing power animal, that can choose to be in whatever dimension it wants.

The qualities and traits that the snow leopard can help us with are:

steadfastness   evolvement   spiritual awareness   generosity of spirit
ability to walk in the footsteps of others
tenaciousness   love of adventure   manifesting

These are the qualities of Source within

However, on our journey of source evolvement and as part of our soul experience we may relate to, or draw towards us, these challenging traits and situations, or subtle echoes of them:

inconstancy   unreliability   parsimony of spiritual giving
hard heartedness   shyness   indecisiveness   limited potential
attracting negativity from others   unappreciated and ingratitude

These are the gifts of grace from Source

Walking in the energy of this power animal will help us to commit to life choices; to stand up and be counted. We will have this power animal with us when we feel weakened by circumstances and need to find that last ounce of strength.

If you resonate with the energy of the snow leopard, you will find that your spiritual growth is the dominating factor in your life. How you choose to balance your life is your choice; however, you can call on the energy of the snow leopard to help you to bring spiritual awareness into every part of your life.

To evolve is to move forward in our understanding of the light beings that we are. This is a soul commitment and will often bring huge soul growth lessons that feel as if we are experiencing the opposite of what we are meant to feel.

The light of the snow leopard helps us to understand what we do not want in order to see clearly what we do want.

Part of 'service to Source' is the generosity of our source self; the need to help others. When we have a connection to the snow leopard it will help us to realise selfless generosity, which is part of unconditional love.

The snow leopard will help us to understand another's life from their perspective. This is a huge enlightening quality as it enables us to be teachers and helpers free from judgement. This is said clearly in the phrase 'Before you judge a man, walk a mile in his shoes.'

True empathy will be a quality that the snow leopard enhances in us.

To be tenacious is a quality that we need when we are using spiritual discipline in our lives, especially when awakening to the awareness of our greater selves.

Being tenacious will help us when perhaps others would give up. It is going that last mile that brings soul growth. However, this can lead to obstinance and perverseness, which is when the energy of this power animal will help us to be tenacious from the wisdom of our source self and not the fearful stubbornness of our personality self.

Manifesting is part of who we are; in its purest form it is limitless Source expressing itself through our three dimensional material self. This is awesome; however, we will often experience the polar opposite of our desired want through the attraction of what we hold in our subconscious mind; our deepest, often unrecognised, anxieties and fears. The snow leopard helps us to manifest from our source self.

It is when we manifest from our source self that we attract what can be described as 'Heaven on Earth'.

The snow leopard will encourage the sense of adventure in us, as well as the need to be free from limitations. Feeling adventurous is a state of being that is free from fear and yet full of anticipation for the expansion of reality. This can lead to soul growth. The snow leopard will walk with us on this journey.

Melchizedek

All That Is: Melchizedek helps us to walk our path with Divine Will and Divine Love. Our spiritual balance evolves within the protection of his sphere of light to bring us nearer to 'all that is'. *Breathe in the power. Breathe in the light, the pure Divine Light of Melchizedek that is all around us and feel his presence.* We are part of the universe and all that is in it. We are finite in our bodies but infinite in our source selves.

Divine Love: Divine Love is life. Life is creation. We create our own thoughts, emotions and actions. We are Divine Love. *Allow yourself to be connected to your own Divine Love through the gratitude and joy in your heart. Recognise the beauty and joy of Divine Love flowing through you.*

Spiritual Balance: This is a way of life, how we approach life as light filled humans. It is how we balance our thoughts, emotions and actions and equally how we balance living in a material world. Know that we are on this planet as a spiritual being having a human experience, rather than a human being having a spiritual experience.

Metatron

Language of the Universe: Metatron helps us to connect to the language of the Universe using numerology, sacred geometry, sound, colours etc. *Ensure that you are well grounded and connect with Metatron to help you to understand the language of the Universe.*

Source within: Metatron guides us to live consciously from our source self in constant awareness of the Source within and without. *Connect with Metatron and his might and clarity to fully connect with the Source within and so move towards enlightenment.*

Oneness: Oneness is the opposite of the illusion of separateness from Source. We are all one. We are all connected to Source and also to each other. The mighty Metatron will help us to fully appreciate the oneness along with the source within.

Sananda

Wisdom: Wisdom is Source filled knowledge. Think about the roles we play in this life as a wise one, a parent, a teacher or guardian, a leader or perhaps in service to others in other ways. We are constantly placed in situations in order to give and receive source filled wisdom. It is in the source energy of light, love and truth that we become our wise self. Awaken to who we are – wise souls.

Peace: Peace is Source. Source is peace. *Call in Sananda and take a few moments to realign with your higher mind, emotions and correctly positioned physical body while experiencing the peace that is in all of us. Let this peace fill your heart and all of your body and aura.*

Deep soul connection: Being deeply soul connected allows us to experience life on Earth as we are meant to, being aware of our challenges in a way that helps us understand our soul growth. This understanding is a deep knowing, which is what makes the challenges 'steps of growth'.

Mary

Unconditional love: Unconditional love is a love free from fear. It is a love free from expectations, a love free from conditions, a love free from judgement. Mary helps us to bring out the compassion, empathy and nurture that is within us, enabling us to live in the moment with unconditional love and forgiveness for ourselves and others.

Forgiveness: Forgiveness is not about condoning an awful deed it is about empathy or metaphorically placing yourself in someone else's shoes and understanding why the situation happened. We also need to forgive ourselves, which is an act of grace. We need to understand, for example, why we hurt someone, or did something that caused them discomfort.

Living in the present: Living in the present moment enables us to connect with Source and to experience pure joy. Living in the present moment, the now, gives us true awareness of our source self. From this space of source awareness we can make clear minded decisions. We can see our fears in a detached manner and understand them with the knowing that comes from source awareness.

Joseph

Steadfast: Joseph was the model of the perfect partner (husband). He was loyal, trusting and infinitely loving, which enabled him to be very grounded and connected, which in turn helps us to be grounded and connected.

Grounded: Joseph is the perfect example of someone who remains very grounded in the material world and yet is still very connected to Source. Being grounded is vitally important to all aspects of life and helps us to be connected and enlightened.

Stability: Joseph is the 'father figure' for today's society. He is dependable, trustworthy, gives stability and he is the first teacher of life skills (which was his role as Jesus's earthly father). We can draw on Joseph's stability to bring stability and the ability to ground into our lives.

Kuthumi

Confidence: When we connect strongly with Source and awaken to the Source within, we become more enlightened, more detached from our lower self or ego self, and more aware of who we are. *Call on Kuthumi to surround you with source light. Hold a piece of carnelian or feel the energy of the crystal in the image; feel the power of Source filling you with confidence and trust in the Source within.*

Connecting from the heart: This is a heart to heart connection. We are in perfect balance when our minds and hearts are working in harmony. *Sit quietly, make sure you are grounded and connected. Feel your strong connection to Source. Focus on your breath, as if breathing from the heart. With each breath feel yourself going further and further into the universe of your heart.*

Higher intuition: This is a deep knowing from our source self; that knowing, inner voice. This is how we receive information from our soul for our greater good, for our soul growth. *Create quiet time every day and allow yourself to connect with the inner voice from your heart. Trust your heart, knowing this is higher intuition.*

Saint Peter

Anchoring Source Energy

Stability: Alongside Joseph, Saint Peter brings stability to all areas of our lives. We can call in Saint Peter whenever we need more stability and wisdom around us.

Keys to your Soul Journey: Saint Peter holds the keys to our Soul Journeys. *Ensure that you are well grounded and connect with him to unlock the next steps on your own unique Soul Journey.*

Rosa (Divine Feminine)

Acceptance: When we accept life and the challenges of living here on planet Earth, we are able to see the life lessons that our challenges are teaching us and Rosa helps us to move forward with love, acceptance and source filled wisdom integrating our life lessons.

Lessons from soulmates: Our soulmates bring us lessons, things we need to know, understand and work with. We can call on Rosa to help us to move forward in our lives, working with and using the lessons that our soulmates bring and so move towards enlightenment with our hearts filled with unconditional love.

Relationships with family: All our relationships are there for a purpose. Our families and friends bring us lessons to learn. We can call in Rosa, ensuring we are well grounded and present in the moment, and work with the insights, messages and lessons that our relationships bring, helping us to enlightenment.

John the Baptist and Saint Germain

Soul journey: The combination of these two words carries the power of Source and the will of Source. Our soul journey is a journey of giving and receiving. This we do with love, blessings and gratitude. These are pure source gifts when they are given and received from the heart.

Clarity: This is seeing from the vision of Source. *Call in the pure light of John the Baptist or Saint Germain to help you to connect with your own source light, your own source clarity and to be guided by your inner source heart.*

Balance and flow: To flow is to create a balance. Flow carries the vibration of movement, and where there is harmonised flow there is equilibrium, which is balance. Calling in John the Baptist or Saint Germain assists in the flow and harmony of life.

Moses

Facing life changes: We all face changes all the time. Changes bring us new possibilities and options. Moses helps us to understand our life changes, integrate the wisdom they bring and to move forward towards enlightenment.

Moving beyond grief: Grief is something we have all had to deal with at some point in our lives. *In these difficult times, call in Moses to help appreciate and understand your feelings and find the strength to integrate the wisdom, value the cause of your grief, move forward through acceptance, with love, wisdom and understanding.*

Authenticity: Moses will guide us to step forward in our power, strength and the inner knowledge from our Source Wisdom, so that we can be our authentic selves. Being our true authentic self is another step towards enlightenment.

Mary Magdalena or Tara

Grounded and connected: Mary Magdalena and Tara help us to use our Divine strength to bring integrity, self empowerment and courage into our lives with an awareness of Source that comes from being grounded, connected and balanced. They are also here to rebalance our lives and our society, thus helping the Earth itself. They are the energetic link between Heaven and Earth, helping us to ground and connect.

Self empowerment: When we approach empowerment from a grounded and connected source filled way, which is the heart felt way, it helps us on our life journey in an empowered way, filled with deep integrity, divine courage, overlit by our own 'divine source self'.

Pure integrity: Allows us to act and speak from a place of strength, and, at times, a place of courage. Allows our higher self to give us further insights into living our life fully in deep, Divine pure integrity. *Call on Mary Magdalena or Tara to help stay grounded and connected, self empowered and work constantly from a place of integrity.*

Maitreya

Help raise vibration: The more we are able to stay grounded and raise our vibrations, the stronger and more connected we become, and the closer we are to enlightenment. Maitreya helps us with this.

Manifestation: *You are the law of attraction and the art of manifestation. Sit with Maitreya, raise your vibration and focus on what you wish to manifest in your life and then let go of the outcome and trust.*

Detachment: Being detached and seeing our life situations from our source self means we are being an observer. Maitreya helps us to manifest, and remain detached from the outcome, bringing trust and peace.

Saint Mikael (Archangel Michael)

Saint Mikael helps us to connect to the love, will and wisdom of Source, that Divine connection that nurtures, supports and inspires us and all areas of our lives.

The love: that pure Divine unconditional love for ourselves and others, trusting our source self and seeing the love in others.

The will: the Divine will leading us forward to on our own unique soul journey with the love and support of Saint Mikael and Source.

The wisdom: the knowing, our connection to Source, enabling us to see the light of Source within ourselves and in others.

Clear Quartz

Clear quartz will amplify, adding strength and emphasis to the image and your understanding of the wisdom it holds. It brings out the beauty within, allowing your talents and gifts to shine. It is also very protective.

Selenite

Selenite brings gentleness, clarity and a lightness within. It helps us to connect to the wisdom and understanding of Source, bringing clarity and clear sight.

Citrine

Citrine is very protective and helps our determination and resolve. It helps us with our deep soul connection as well as bringing us peace and understanding.

Rose Quartz

Rose quartz connects us to unconditional love and helps us to live in the present moment in harmony, with a love for life and all the positive things it offers.

Malachite

Malachite brings stability and is grounding. It also helps to reveal what we need to release in order to move forward.

Carnelian

Carnelian strengthens our confidence and our heart connection to Source, energising us and helping us to manifest our Divine way forward using our intuition.

Desert Rose

Desert rose connects to wise, ancient knowledge, helping us to move forward on our own unique soul journey with grounded stability and wisdom.

Blue Lace Agate

Blue lace agate brings clarity and blessings, helping us to move forward in the flow of pure source energy.

Red Jasper

Red jasper helps our inner strength, so that we can be our authentic selves and face life changes with love and wisdom.

Labradorite

Labradorite helps us to be grounded and connected, as it strengthens our connection to source wisdom, self empowerment and Divine Love.

Amethyst

Amethyst raises our vibration and brings us strength and wisdom, which in turn helps us to manifest. It is also very protective.

Moonstone

Moonstone is the stone of new beginnings, and has the effect of calming the emotions.

Visualisation to work with the Power Animals

The Power Animals that work specifically with these Guidance Images are:

Blue Whale	**One**	**Goldfinch and Eagle**	**Two**
Doves	**Three**	**Deer**	**Four**
Jaguar	**Five**	**Swan**	**Six**
Dolphin	**Seven**	**Tiger & Red Admiral Butterfly**	**Eight**
White Husky and Hare	**Nine**	**Snow Leopard**	**Eleven**

The power animals help us to work with our soul contract, highlighting what we need to focus on in this lifetime, the promises we have made to our soul, to the universe.

What we are working on in this lifetime can be seen as a magnifying glass on the current part of our soul journey.

The power animal can also help us with our daily challenges in life, which can be seen as soul growth opportunities.

We recommend that you record the following power animal visualisation on your phone or other medium, so that you can relax and listen to the words; also hearing your own voice leading the visualisation is very empowering.

Decide which power animal you would like to work with at this time and study the image relevant to that power animal (the list above will direct you to the relevant numbered image for that power animal).

If your power animal is water based, for instance the dolphins, know that you are perfectly safe in the water, surrounded by a pure sphere of energy ensuring that you can breathe freely and easily.

Sit quietly where you will not be disturbed. Take some deep relaxing diaphragm breaths and reinforce your strong connection with Mother Earth, then reinforce your strong connection to Source, to God, to the Divine.

Take some more relaxing diaphragm breaths to help you connect with your chosen power animal. You may like to imagine yourself in the countryside, or by the water where your power animal will be found.

Be aware of your power animal moving closer to you until it is beside you. Feel very comfortable and at peace in its presence.

Ask your chosen power animal to help you to move forward on your own unique soul journey by highlighting what you need to focus on in this lifetime, the promises you have made to your soul, to the universe; or helping you with your current challenges in life.

Sit quietly and absorb the insights, information that this wonderful power animal is helping you with.

How can you integrate these insights into your life to help you to move forward easily and smoothly?

What else does the power animal need you to know at the moment?

Visualise your life with these insights fully integrated.

In your own time, when you are ready, thank the power animal, thank Mother Earth and Source and take some relaxing diaphragm breaths and feel yourself sitting quietly on the chair. Bring your attention back into the room and when you are ready, open your eyes, take a drink of water and record any insights, messages or inspirations that you have received.

Visualisation to work with one of the Masters

The table on page 6 details the Masters that work with these Images.

Melchizedek	One	Metatron	Two
Sananda	Three	Mary and Joseph	Four
Kuthumi	Five	St Peter and Rosa	Six
John the Baptist and Saint Germain	Seven	Moses	Eight
Mary Magdalena and Tara	Nine	Maitreya	Eleven

Each of the images has an ascended master who works closely to help and assist. You may like to work with the master connected to your soul journey or soul contract. Alternatively you can work with any of the masters to give you inspiration, insights and wisdom.

We suggest that you record the visualisation so that you can relax and enjoy all aspects and get maximum benefit from the messages you receive.

Find a quiet space where you will not be disturbed. Take some relaxing diaphragm breaths and feel your strong connection to Mother Earth, so that you are well grounded. Then feel your strong connection to Source, God, the Divine, so that you are well grounded and well connected.

Take some more relaxing diaphragm breaths and take yourself to a beautiful place in nature. A place where you feel comfortable and relaxed. This may be a place that you are familiar with or a new amazing space.

Look around you and drink in the beauty and the wonder of this incredible place. What can you see around you? Are there trees, bushes, grass, birds, flowers? What does the sky look like? How do you feel? Be aware of the mighty Divine presence approaching you. Relax and be open to the inspirations, insights and wisdom that you are going to receive.

As the master gets closer to you, they are smiling and very happy to see you. Look into their eyes and drink in the magic and the Divinity.

Quietly in your own way ask for the help and support that you need and be open to the messages that you receive.

What else does the master want you to know?

How can you integrate this into your life?

Do you have any other questions for the master?

Does the master have any other messages for you?

In your own time, when you are ready, thank the master, Source and Mother Earth and take some relaxing diaphragm breaths. Gently being your attention back into the room, feel yourself sitting comfortably on the chair, still well grounded and present in the moment. When you are ready, gently open your eyes, have a drink of water and make any notes that will help you integrate this wisdom and understanding.

Visualisation to work with your Soul Journey Image

There are two stages relating to your soul journey, as detailed on page 12.

This visualisation will help you with both stages of your soul journey, helping and supporting you, giving you insights and inspirations.

We recommend that you work with each stage of your journey separately, recording this visualisation so that you can relax and enjoy all aspects.

Have the relevant soul journey image in front of you.

Take some deep relaxing diaphragm breaths and feel your strong connection with Mother Earth, so that you are well grounded. Then feel your strong connection to Source, God, the Divine, so that you are connected and grounded.

Feel your body relaxing as it absorbs the wisdom and assistance from Mother Earth and Source.

Be aware of your chosen image. Call in the power animal that works with this image. Take your time to be present with this magnificent creature and acknowledge their wisdom and help.

Be aware of the master that is connected with the image and how this master is guiding and inspiring you on your soul journey.

Visualise the sacred shape around you, feel all aspects of it and the inspirations you are receiving.

Become aware of the appropriate crystal and colour associated with your chosen image.

Be aware of all aspects of your image, how they are working together to help you progress on your soul journey.

Sit quietly and absorb the messages and insights that you are receiving.

Is there anything else you need to know about your soul journey at this time?

Do you have any questions?

Is there anything else you need to be aware of at this time?

Is there anything else that will be helpful and supportive to you?

In your own time, when you are ready, thank the power animal, the shape, the master, crystal and colour for all their support, their wisdom and their knowing.

Take a few relaxing diaphragm breaths and gently bring your attention back into the room, feel yourself sitting comfortably on the chair still well connected, grounded and present in the moment. When you are ready, gently open your eyes, have a drink of water and make any necessary notes.

Visualisation to work with your Soul Contract Image

Our soul contract highlights what we need to focus on in this lifetime, the promise we have made to our soul, to the universe. What we are working on in this lifetime can be seen as a magnifying glass on the current part of our soul journey.

This visualisation will help you to move forward in this lifetime, releasing the fears and challenges that hold you back on your soul journey, thereby helping and supporting you, giving you insights and inspirations to move forward. Helping you to find the harmony and peace within.

We recommend that you work with your soul contract image and the appropriate power animal by recording this visualisation so that you can relax and enjoy all aspects.

Have the relevant soul journey image in front of you.

Take some deep relaxing diaphragm breaths and feel your strong connection with Mother Earth, so that you are well grounded. Then feel your strong connection to Source, God, the Divine, so that you are connected and grounded.

Feel your body relaxing as it absorbs the wisdom and assistance from Mother Earth and Source.

Be aware of your chosen image and all that is held within it. Call in the power animal that works with this image. Take your time to absorb the energy of this magnificent creature and acknowledge their wisdom and help.

This image is helping and supporting you with your soul contract, your focus for this lifetime. Be open and present to the wisdom and knowing that you are being shown.

Are there any fears or challenges that are being cleared and transmuted for you so that you can move forward more easily and smoothly?

Is there anything you need to do to help this process?

Are there any further insights that will help to move you forward into a positive, fulfilling life?

Become aware of the peace and harmony within and around you.

Is there anything else you need to know about your soul contract at this time?

In your own time, when you are ready, thank Source, Mother Earth and the power animal for all their support, their wisdom and their knowing.

Take a few relaxing diaphragm breaths and gently bring your attention back into the room, feel yourself sitting comfortably on the chair still well connected and present in the moment. When you are ready, gently open your eyes, have a drink of water and make any necessary notes.

Visualisation to work with an Active Awareness Image

There are six active awareness images (sacred shapes)

The Sphere	**The Pyramid**
The Octahedron	**The Star Tetrahedron**
The Twelve Pointed Star	**The Seed of Life**

We suggest that you spend time with each of these active awareness images as they carry the vibration of a sacred source geometric shape. You may feel drawn to connecting with the appropriate shape through a visualisation. You may then feel drawn to keeping the shape around you for the rest of the day, and noting how your day has progressed and been helped and supported by the energy of that shape.

We recommend that you record the visualisation on your phone or other device so that you can relax and listen to it without interruption. It is always very powerful to listen to your own voice leading you through a visualisation.

Have the relevant active awareness image in front of you.

Take some deep relaxing diaphragm breaths and feel your strong connection with Mother Earth, so that you are well grounded. Then feel your strong connection to Source, God, the Divine, so that you are both connected and grounded.

Feel your body relaxing as it absorbs the wisdom and knowledge from Source and Mother Earth.

Be aware of the active awareness image and the wonderful shape that it shows.

Relax and absorb the shape around you.

How does it feel? What inspirations and insights are you receiving?

Be aware of the peace and harmony within you.

You may feel drawn to keeping the shape around you for the rest of the day.

In your own time, when you are ready, thank Source, Mother Earth and the active awareness sacred shape for all their support, their wisdom and their understanding.

Take a few relaxing diaphragm breaths and gently bring your attention back into the room, feel yourself sitting comfortably on the chair still well connected and present in the moment. When you are ready, gently open your eyes, have a drink of water and make any necessary notes.

Visualisation to work with the Past Lives

We recommend that you read through this visualisation so that you are very familiar with it and then record it (it is always very powerful to hear your own voice leading you through a visualisation). Look at the active awareness images.

Sit quietly and take some deep relaxing diaphragm breaths, connect to Mother Earth, so that you feel well grounded, then connect to Source, God, the Divine, so that you have a strong, connection. Take some more deep relaxing diaphragm breaths with the awareness that you are tuning into a past life to help you in this lifetime, use the methods on page 10, 11 and 114 and select the appropriate image.

With your chosen image, study all the features on it and read the relevant page relating to that image. If one of the images relates to the number seven, then you are working with the gifts that you have brought forward from a past life, and the sacred shape, the seed of life, will assist you.

If your image relates to a number other than seven, then the relevant past life is telling you what you need to know, which is the starting point of what happened and how it relates to this lifetime. The sacred shape, the twelve pointed star, will help and support you here.

Study your chosen image. Read the relevant pages in the book. Absorb the energy of the twelve pointed star if you are working with the majority of the images in the book, or the seed of life if you are working with one of the number seven images.

Sit quietly, close your eyes, bring your attention to the present moment and take some deep relaxing diaphragm breaths. Visualise the appropriate shape around you – either the twelve pointed star or the seed of life. When you are very comfortable with this shape around you, then call in the help and support of the snow leopard.

When you are ready, become aware of your chosen image and let the wisdom, understanding and knowledge to flow easily and smoothly to you helping and supporting you on your own unique soul journey, your journey towards enlightenment, your journey for this lifetime. You may also be aware of the seeds that you have brought with you from past lives and how you can integrate and use them within this lifetime.

Take your time to fully experience this wonderful, life enhancing time.

When you are ready, in your own time, thank the sacred shape that you have been working with, as well as the power animal, Mother Earth and Source.

Take a few deep relaxing diaphragm breaths, feel yourself still well grounded and present in the moment, and gently bring your attention back into the room, feel yourself sitting comfortably on the chair and when you are ready open your eyes and make a note of your experience, the help and guidance you have received and the wisdom you are bringing forward.

ONE

I

COMPLETION BRINGING
NEW BEGINNINGS

TWO

II

SOURCE AND
PERSONALITY SELF

THREE

III

LOVE, WILL AND WISDOM IN THE MOMENT

THREE

source energy pattern

ONE + TWO

I + II

FAMILY
INTERACTIONS

FOUR

IV

CONNECTING WITH MOTHER EARTH

JILLY STOTT AND LESLÉ AYRE | 174

FOUR

source energy pattern

ONE + THREE

I + III

REGENERATE AND REJUVENATE
WITH NATURE

FOUR

source energy pattern

TWO+TWO

II+II

TRUST YOUR
SOURCE SELF

FIVE

LOVE YOURSELF

FIVE

source energy pattern

ONE + FOUR

I+IV

WE ARE BEINGS OF LIGHT

FIVE

source energy pattern

TWO + THREE

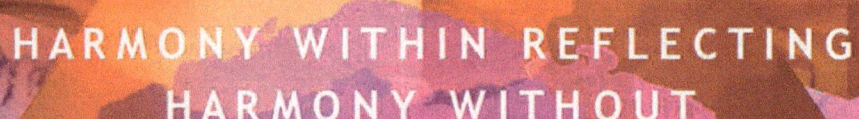

HARMONY WITHIN REFLECTING
HARMONY WITHOUT

SIX

VI

PARENT CHILD RELATIONSHIP

SIX

source energy pattern

ONE+FIVE

BE MINDFUL OF
THE PRESENT

SIX

source energy pattern

TWO + FOUR

II + IV

LESSONS FROM SOULMATES

SIX

source energy pattern

THREE + THREE

III + III

ACCEPT AND
MOVE FORWARD

SEVEN

VII

ATTENTION TO
THE BREATH

SEVEN

source energy pattern

ONE + SIX

I+VI

WATER'S HEALING
POWERS

SEVEN

source energy pattern

TWO + FIVE

II + V

WE ARE ALL
HEALERS

SEVEN

source energy pattern

THREE + FOUR

III + IV

AWAKEN YOUR
PASSION FOR LIFE

EIGHT

VIII

FACING LIFE CHANGES

EIGHT

source energy pattern

ONE + SEVEN

I + VII

RESISTANCE TO CHANGE

EIGHT

source energy pattern

TWO + SIX

II + VI

MOVING
BEYOND GRIEF

EIGHT

source energy pattern

THREE + FIVE

III + V

BE
AUTHENTIC

EIGHT

source energy pattern

FOUR+FOUR

IV+IV

RECEIVING WHAT YOU CREATE

NINE

IX

FIND YOUR
CORE PURPOSE

NINE

source energy pattern

ONE+EIGHT

XVIII

JOURNEY OF
SELF DISCOVERY

NINE

source energy pattern

TWO + SEVEN

II + VII

READY TO MAKE A
LIFE COMMITMENT

NINE

source energy pattern

THREE + SIX

III + VI

A SIGN FROM
THE UNIVERSE

N I N E

source energy pattern

FOUR + FIVE

IV+V

SPIRITUAL
DISCIPLINE

ELEVEN

XI

YOU ARE THE
LAW OF ATTRACTION

JILLY STOTT AND LESLÉ AYRE

ELEVEN

source energy pattern

TWO + NINE

II + IX

THE ART OF
MANIFESTATION

ELEVEN

source energy pattern

THREE+EIGHT

II+VII
+V

BE AN OBSERVER

ELEVEN

source energy pattern

FOUR + SEVEN

IV + VII

RAISING YOUR VIBRATION

ELEVEN
source energy pattern
FIVE + SIX
V+VI
APPRECIATION LEADS TO HAPPINESS
JILLY STOTT AND LESLÉ AYRE | 202

ACTIVE
AWARENESS

SPHERE

You are called to work with this shape

ACTIVE
AWARENESS

PYRAMID
You are called to work with this shape

ACTIVE
AWARENESS

OCTAHEDRON
You are called to work with this shape

ACTIVE
AWARENESS
———

STAR TETRAHEDRON
You are called to work with this shape

JILLY STOTT AND LESLÉ AYRE | 206

ACTIVE
AWARENESS

TWELVE POINTED STAR

You are called to work with this shape

ACTIVE
AWARENESS

SEED OF LIFE
You are called to work with this shape

Index

Inspiration for the book by Jilly Stott i

Introduction 1

Soul Journey Numbers Book – your guide towards enlightenment 2

    Soul journey numbers 2

The numeric patterns of source energy within each number 3

    Numeric patterns of source energy 3

Principal numbers one, two and three 4

Soul journey and soul contract 4

    Soul journey 4

    Soul contract 5

What to notice on each Soul Journey Guidance image 6

    The power animals 7

    The white owl 8

    Active awareness Sacred Shapes 8

    Masters 8

    Crystals 8

    Colours 8

Using the Soul Journey Guidance Images 9

Method one: intuitive inspiration for the day 10

How to use the Soul Journey Guidance Images Intuitively 10

Chart to choose your appropriate image 11

Method two: soul journey (stage one and two) 12

    Calculate your Soul Journey Number stage one 12

    Double numbers and their significance 13

    If your soul journey/contract number ends in a zero or a single digit 13

    How to understand your soul journey number 14

    Working with the first stage of your soul journey 14

    Working with the second stage of your soul journey 15

Method three: soul contract number 16

    To calculate your soul contract number 16

Soul journey guidance one 17

Soul journey guidance two 19

Soul journey guidance three 21

    Soul journey three: source energy pattern one+two 23

Soul journey guidance four 25
    Soul journey four: source energy pattern one+three 27
    Soul journey four: source energy pattern two+two 29

Soul journey guidance five 31
    Soul journey five: source energy pattern one+four 33
    Soul journey source energy pattern two+three 35

Soul journey guidance six 37
    Soul journey six: source energy pattern one+five 39
    Soul journey six: source energy pattern two+four 41
    Soul journey six: source energy pattern three+three 43

Soul Growth journey seven 45
    Soul journey seven: source energy pattern one+six 47
    Soul journey seven: source energy pattern two+five 49
    Soul journey seven: source energy pattern three+four 51

Soul journey guidance eight 53
    Soul journey eight: source energy pattern one+seven 55
    Soul journey eight: source energy pattern two+six 57
    Soul journey eight: source energy pattern three+five 59
    Soul journey eight: source energy pattern four+four 61

Soul journey guidance nine 63
    Soul journey nine: source energy pattern one+eight 65
    Soul journey nine: source energy pattern two+seven 67
    Soul journey nine: source energy pattern three+six 69
    Soul journey nine: source energy pattern four+five 71

Soul journey guidance eleven 73
    Soul journey eleven: source energy pattern two+nine 75
    Soul journey eleven: source energy pattern three+eight 77
    Soul journey eleven: source energy pattern four+seven 79
    Soul journey eleven: source energy pattern five+six 82

Method four: soul journey birth day numbers 84
    If your birth day energy is the number one 85
    If your birth day energy is the number two 86
    If your birth day energy is the number three 87
    If your birth day energy is the number four 88
    If your birth day energy is the number five 89
    If your birth day energy is the number six 90
    If your birth day energy is the number seven 91
    If your birth day energy is the number eight 92
    If your birth day energy is the number nine 93
    If your birth day energy is the number eleven 94

Method five: how your name supports your individual soul journey 95
    Names 95
    Look at the name you are known by 97
    Summary of how to use your name to support yourself 100
    Looking at the core resonance of your name 100

Intuitive Inspirations
    Number one Intuitive Inspirations 101
    Number two Intuitive Inspirations 102
    Number three Intuitive Inspirations 103
    Number four Intuitive Inspirations 104
    Number five Intuitive Inspirations 105
    Number six Intuitive Inspirations 106
    Number seven Intuitive Inspirations 107
    Number eight Intuitive Inspirations 108
    Number nine Intuitive Inspirations 109
    Number eleven Intuitive Inspirations 110

Method six: further insights using month and year numbers 111
    To calculate the year number 111
    To calculate the month number 111

Method seven: working with the power animals 111

Method eight: working with the sacred shapes 111

Method nine: working with past lives 112
    Method A Working with the Seed of Life 112
    Method B Working with the Twelve Pointed Star 113

    Selecting your soul guidance image from the code 114

Active awareness 115
    Active awareness sphere 116
    Active awareness pyramid – four sided pyramid with a square base 118
    Active awareness octahedron 120
    Active awareness star tetrahedron – consisting of two tetrahedra 122
    Active awareness twelve pointed star – stellated dodecahedron 124
    Active awareness the seed of life - seven interlocking spheres 126

Further insights on the numbers 128
    Number one   further insights 128
    Number two   further insights 129
    Number three further insights 130
    Number four further insights 131
    Number five further insights 132
    Number six further insights 133
    Number seven further insights 134
    Number eight further insights 135

Number nine further insights 136
Number eleven further insights 137

Power animals
Power animal: blue whale 138
Power animal: golden eagle and goldfinch 140
Power animal: three doves 142
Power animal: deer (stag and doe) 144
Power animal: jaguar 146
Power animal: swan (cob and pen) 148
Power animal: dolphin 150
Power animal: tiger and red admiral butterfly 152
Power animal: white husky 154
Power animal: the hare 155
Power animal: snow leopard 156

Masters
Melchizedek 158
Metatron 158
Sananda 158
Mary 159
Joseph 159
Kuthumi 159
Saint Peter 160
Rosa (Divine Feminine) 160
John the Baptist and Saint Germain 160
Moses 160
Mary Magdalena or Tara 161
Maitreya 161
Saint Mikael (Archangel Michael) 161

Crystals
Clear Quartz 162
Selenite 162
Citrine 162
Rose Quartz 162
Malachite 162
Carnelian 162
Desert Rose 162
Blue Lace Agate 162
Red Jasper 162
Labradorite 162
Amethyst 162
Moonstone 162

Visualisation to work with the power animal 163
Visualisation to work with one of the masters 165
Visualisation to work with your soul journey image 166
Visualisation to work with your soul contract image 167

Visualisation to work with an Active Awareness image 168
Visualisation to work with past lives 169

Soul guidance images:
    One   170
    Two   171
    Three 172
    Three (1+2) 173
    Four   174
    Four (1+3) 175
    Four (2+2) 176
    Five   177
    Five (1+4) 178
    Five (2+3) 179
    Six 180
    Six (1+5) 181
    Six (2+4) 182
    Six (3+3) 183
    Seven 184
    Seven (1+6) 185
    Seven (2+5) 186
    Seven (3+4) 187
    Eight 188
    Eight (1+7) 189
    Eight (2+6) 190
    Eight (3+5) 191
    Eight (4+4) 192
    Nine 193
    Nine (1+8) 194
    Nine (2+7) 195
    Nine (3+6) 196
    Nine (4+5) 197
    Eleven 198
    Eleven (2+9) 199
    Eleven (3+8) 200
    Eleven (4+7) 201
    Eleven (5+6) 202

Active awareness images
    Active awareness sphere 203
    Active awareness pyramid – four sided pyramid with a square base 204
    Active awareness octahedron 205
    Active awareness star tetrahedron – consisting of two tetrahedra 206
    Active awareness twelve pointed star – stellated dodecahedron 207
    Active awareness the seed of life - seven interlocking spheres 208

Owl Picture 209
Index 210

Milton Keynes UK
Ingram Content Group UK Ltd.
UKHW021935071124
450833UK00009B/80

9 781962 987714